WORLD'S END:
2009

WORLD'S END:
2009

PROPHECIES FOR THE COMING
MESSIAH AND ARMAGEDDON

PETER LORIE

JEREMY P. TARCHER / PENGUIN
a member of Penguin Group (USA) Inc.
New York

My thanks first and foremost to Sandra Delaney for her skills as an editor and researcher. This was a complex book to create, and her precision and exact, academic ability made it all possible.

JEREMY P. TARCHER/PENGUIN
Published by the Penguin Group
www.penguin.com
Penguin Group (USA) Inc., 375 Hudson Street, New York, New York 10014, USA
Penguin Group (Canada), 10 Alcorn Avenue, Toronto, Ontario, Canada M4V 3B2
(a division of Pearson Penguin Canada Inc.)
Penguin Books Ltd, 80 Strand, London WC2R 0RL, England
Penguin Ireland, 25 St Stephen's Green, Dublin 2, Ireland
(a division of Penguin Books Ltd)
Penguin Group (Australia), 250 Camberwell, Victoria 3124, Australia (a division of
Pearson Australia Group Pty Ltd)
Penguin Books India Pvt Ltd, 11 Community Centre, Panchsheel Park,
New Delhi–110 017, India
Penguin Group (NZ), Cnr Airborne and Rosedale Roads, Albany, Auckland 1310,
New Zealand (a division of Pearson New Zealand Ltd)
Penguin Books (South Africa) (Pty) Ltd, 24 Sturdee Avenue, Rosebank, Johannesburg
2196, South Africa
Penguin Books Ltd, Registered Offices: 80 Strand, London, WC2R 0RL, England

Most Tarcher/Penguin books are available at special quantity discounts for bulk purchase for sales promotions, premiums, fund-raising, and educational needs. Special books or book excerpts also can be created to fit specific needs. For details, write Penguin Group (USA) Inc. Special Markets, 375 Hudson Street, New York, NY 10014.

All quotations from the Bible are from the King James Version, unless otherwise indicated.

While the author has made every effort to provide accurate telephone numbers and Internet addresses at the time of publication, neither the publisher nor the author assumes any responsibility for errors, or for changes that occur after publication.

The Library of Congress cataloged the hardcover edition as follows:

Lorie, Peter.
World's end, 2009 : prophecies for the coming Messiah and Armageddon / Peter Lorie.
p. cm.
Includes bibliographical references and index.
ISBN 1-58542-284-3
1. End of the world. 2. Bible—Prophecies. I. Title.
BT877.L67   2004   2003063381
236'.9—dc22

ISBN 1-58542-385-8 (paperback edition)

Printed in the United States of America
1 3 5 7 9 10 8 6 4 2

Book design by Gretchen Achilles

TO MY SON BENJAMIN.
NO MORE COULD A SON BE.

CONTENTS

INTRODUCTION

In June 1987, I turned on the television in my home in Italy and watched a news program that related a potential conflict between General Khaddafi and the US fleet in the Mediterranean. It was another confrontative event between two countries, another news story indicating that human beings are unable to be at peace with each other—no big deal. But for me it *was* a big deal, because six months before, I had translated and interpreted a verse from the prophecies of Nostradamus, the sixteenth-century prophet, that outlined this exact sequence of events in the future. In effect, I knew this event was going to occur in all its detail, for Nostradamus had revealed as much in one four-line verse written four hundred and fifty years earlier.

In September 2001, I watched the catastrophic events in New York City as the Twin Towers tumbled to the ground and thousands of people were murdered by the madness of one group of lunatics. Ten years before this event I had translated and interpreted another of Nostradamus' verses and various lines from the Book of Revelation, which predicted this event and the surrounding circumstances. Sadly, Nostradamus got the date wrong by two years and two months (not bad from over four hundred fifty years in the past), but his description of a "terrible force from the sky over New York" was precisely accurate in every other way as far as any prophecy can be.

THE TRUTH OF PROPHECY. DO WE KNOW IT?

As with every form of genuine prophecy that established and proven prophets have written in our past, predictions involve layers of meaning. Because of pressure from the Catholic Church's Inquisition, the prophecies of Nostradamus were disguised, formatted, and expressed in several languages, with the use of complex symbolism, astrology, numerology, and even conundrums. The biblical prophets undoubtedly used similar methods and added hidden mysteries and parables that may have been familiar to the writers, thousands of years ago, but which may be quite unfamiliar to modern interpreters. We may be hindered in our understanding not just because we lack information about ancient methods but because we are unable to step outside our own belief systems in interpreting ancient texts. A parable or story may seem to have an obvious meaning to us in our cultural and historical context but which could well be the wrong meaning, because the story contains information relevant to another time and place.

The grand periods of astrological change provide us with a contemporary system dictated by the conditioning and psychology they evoke, and this is applicable to every age. The factual, geographical, and historical knowledge of each age changes in many factors during the following age. And this is not just so within the grand astrological eras, but from one period of history to another. Nostradamus, therefore, used his own "local" historical or geographic knowledge to write the disguised prophecy that we, in our age, must figure out.

The prediction of 9/11 envisioned by Nostradamus hundreds of years in advance is a good example of this. The text of the prediction reads as follows:

The year 1999 and seven months, from the skies will come a great and frightening king, to bring back the great King of Angoulmois, before/after Mars is to reign through happiness.[1]

Until the events in New York, this quatrain was most often interpreted as meaning that the world was somehow going to end in 1999. This is one of the very few verses that contains an actual predicted date. If we take into account the fact that Nostradamus was often wrong about his dates (including those that did not contain actual figures but astrological references) by a year or two, we can easily apply this quatrain to September 11, 2001. But where is the connection with New York or Manhattan Island?

The first, most important part of this verse is the reference to "Angoulmois," for this brings us back to our suggestion that many prophetic verses contain words that are historically sourced. Most interpreters understand the name "Angoulmois" in relation only to its relevance in the Middle Ages, so this is where we will begin our hunt.

During Nostradamus' early years, a man named Giovanni da Verrazano served the French king Francis I from 1515 to 1547. Francis I also happened to be Count of Angoulême, the region being part of the possessions of the French royal dynasty of Valois.

In around 1524, when Nostradamus was eighteen, Verrazano traveled a very long distance to a remote island off the coast of a country that had been visited some years earlier by Christopher Columbus. Verrazano called this island Angoulême after his master's title, Count of Angoulême. It later became known as Manhattan Island. One of the bridges leading out of Manhattan is named after the island's founder—the Verrazano Bridge.

Nostradamus would have known all about "Angouleme," and if we believe in his powers of "sight," he would have had at least some idea about what this small island was going to turn out to be some years later. This effectively connects the prediction at the beginning of this section with New York's Manhattan Island.

So we have a "terrifying" leader (in this case Bin Laden) likely to appear from the sky perhaps between 1999 and 2001 over New York City, which will "bring back" the city (Angoulmois/Manhattan). The reference to "bring back" may seem confusing until we look at the way Nostradamus frequently mixes metaphors, descriptions, and meanings. "Bring back" is simply a way of guiding the mind into the mode of the words. It's a bit like saying "bring back your thoughts to Angoulême."

So all this sounds pretty accurate, even though the date was two years off. Unfortunately, none of the interpreters of Nostradamus had connected Angoulmois to Manhattan Island, so no one understood this quatrain to foretell an attack on Manhattan from the air.

This extraordinary single prophecy gives us a clear idea of how texts can be unclear because we fail to read prophecy from the point of view of the time of the prophet. The necessity of looking at the approaches and understanding of ancient prophets will be one of the founding bases of our look at the biblical prophecies concerning the arrival of a Messiah and the potential for our world that can result.

Prophets in our modern age, such as Edgar Cayce and Jeane Dixon, have also had a fair rate of success in their visions of futures during their lifetimes. One of the most notorious examples was Jeane Dixon's prediction of the assassination of John F. Kennedy. She even attempted to warn the Kennedy family of their fate but was paid scant attention. Like almost all other successful prophets, Jeane Dixon attributed her success to a spiritual source. Cayce was also quite successful in short-term predictions. He predicted the rise of Hitler, World War II, India's independence from Britain, the rebirth of Israel as a nation, and the discovery of the community near the Dead Sea, keepers of the Dead Sea scrolls.

THE TRUTH OF PROPHECY

Given a plethora of doubt, particularly in this scientific age of "provable" concepts, how do we know when a prophecy is true? The older format of establishing truth in such matters was the "self-fulfilling" nature of the process. A prophecy from the Bible was the word of God if it proved accurate. In his book *The Late Great Planet Earth*, Hal Lindsey said:

> *A question was asked of Moses that is still being asked today. "How may we know the word which the Lord has spoken? [Deuteronomy 18:21]. And Moses gave the answer—the true test of a prophet: "When a prophet speaks in the name of the Lord, if the word does not come to pass or come true, that is a word which the Lord has not spoken" (Deut. 18:22).[2]*

First and foremost, we must understand that not all prophecy is accurate, even prophecy from the Bible. Errors in transcription, false interpretations, and genuine mistakes all contribute to the fact that not everything spoken in the name of God is necessarily accurate or even meant to be taken literally. Additionally, many of the prophecies in the Bible have already been applied to past events. Not everything written down in the Holy Book is relevant to the twentieth and twenty-first centuries. The number of prophecies in the Bible that have reached fulfillment is overwhelming, and provides proof of the potential accuracy of those prophecies that remain unfulfilled today. For example, prophets successfully predicted the invasion of Jerusalem by the Babylonians, the destruction of the first Temple, and the captivity of the people. Others then predicted the release of the Hebrews and the rebuilding of the Temple. The defilement of the Temple by Antiochus Epiphanes for three and a half years, as well as the destruction of the second Temple, was also predicted. Christians believe that the birth, life, and death of Jesus fulfilled many Hebrew prophecies, and in modern times, many believe that the reestablishment of Israel as a nation, into which Jews from all the nations are gathered, is a fulfillment of biblical prophecy.

Our tendency toward cynical disbelief, due to the age we live in, has diminished the chances that we will accept a single prophecy today. This, plus the fact that the majority of people have no interest in reading the Bible, let alone studying it closely, has brought us to a point where we simply cast aside the potential of biblical prophecy in favor of ignorance of it. Who among the readers of this book could claim even general knowledge of biblical material? We've simply lost interest in this glorious work of genius and spiritual truth. There are many other scriptural tracts available to us now—in the East, for example, where other works of great scripture have become more fashionable or exciting to people in this age. However, the Bible does a far better job of seeing the future than any other spiritual scripture of any age. In fact, it is truly awesome in this respect.

In this book, we will discover the real potential of biblical prophecy, and we will look at this prophecy from the point of view of the ancient prophets, instead of imposing twenty-first-century perspectives or the understanding of European Christianity of the Middle Ages. We must understand these prophets on their own terms, and only then can we gain full access to their amazing message.

We are going to look at the way the ancients understood the meaning of numbers and form, and the symbolic nature of number, including units of time. Next, we will look at how myth was used by the ancients, particularly in the images of the Beasts of Revelation and other biblical prophecies. This will give us a surprising insight into the relationship between the Antichrist and Jesus.

We will look closely at popular ideas about what will happen in the End Time and examine what the scriptures really say. Does the Temple in Jerusalem need to be rebuilt before the Messiah can come? Is the Apocalypse yet to come? Has the battle of Armageddon already happened, and, if not, who will fight in it? Who are Gog and Magog, and how do they fit into the story? Do we play a role in determining when the Messiah will return? What is the spiritual renewal biblical prophecy talks about?

Who is the Messiah, and what will happen when he returns? Most important, do we have a clue as to when the Messiah will return? We believe that the time of the return of the Messiah depends in part on whether we are ready for the spiritual renewal that makes us prepared to receive the Messiah. There are reoccurring cycles of apocalypse and renewal in which the Messiah can return if humanity is ready. If humanity is not ready, each successive cycle of apocalypse is more severe than the last. The next could destroy life as we know it.

The twentieth century was a time of apocalypse that culminated with the establishment of Israel the nation as a force to be reckoned with in the world. This is a significant event in biblical prophecy and signals major events to come. Both biblical and other prophecy point to this as a time of transition and choice. We can choose renewal or apocalypse.

A crucial date in this calculation is the year 2009. We understand Revelation to foretell a significant event happening forty-two years after the return of Israel. Though Israel was formally established earlier, its security as a nation was established in the Six Day War of 1967. Prophecy indicates that the course of this round of apocalypse will be determined by the year 2009.

Will this be a time of great spiritual renewal? Will this be the end of life as we know it? Will the Messiah return? As John says in the Book of Revelation, this is a time for us to wake up, make sure our lamps are full of oil, and be prepared to meet the bridegroom.

—PETER LORIE

CHAPTER 1

AN OVERVIEW OF PROPHECY

THE UNPOPULAR TRUTH OF THE FUTURE

The other major problem of prophecy is that it tends to make the proponent of it unpopular, as the future is not always what we want it to be. We may dream of utopia or of watching people we don't like struck down by God, but truth rarely matches our expectations. We love to hear both good news and horrifying news. We love to be flattered. We prefer to be told that in the future we will win the good fight or succeed in our ventures, but this may not be what we actually need to hear. Dreams come from the mind of humanity, while truth and reality arise from the universe or God, and this truth is uncompromising. Thus it is inevitable that the prophets are frequently unpopular.

There are many examples of this, and prophets have suffered as a result. Jeremiah's prophecy that Nebuchadnezzar would vanquish Judah, that the Jewish survivors of the attack would be imprisoned, and what the length of their imprisonment and enslavement would be brought great anger from his people—not unnaturally. But was he right? Modern archaeologists have proven him to be quite accurate. The Jewish people have preserved his prophecies, because their fulfillment has revealed them to be the word of God.

Prophets are, of course, in particular danger if their unpopular predictions come to fulfillment in their own lifetimes. Even if they don't, the prophet can suffer if his prophecies are not acceptable to the political climate of the time. There have been others than Jeremiah who have not only made unpopular prophecies but have found them fulfilled before their own deaths. And the fulfillment of a prophecy does not always bring the prophet to fame and fortune. Nostradamus was one of those who not only predicted events during his lifespan but also suffered because they came to fruition.

Nostradamus found himself in difficulty on a number of occasions because unpopular predictions came true—predicting the death of the French King Henry II, the fate of the Valois line of Catherine de Medici, and numerous other smaller events. In consequence, he incurred Catherine's and Henry's distinct disapproval and was accused of heresy by the Inquisition. He spent many years on the run, hunted like a criminal by the Inquisition.

This also happened to other biblical prophets, whose prophecies were fulfilled during their lifetimes. Isaiah is a good example of success in all areas of prophecy. His work was not only accurate locally during his lifetime but was also accurate globally for a period of two hundred years beyond his lifetime, such as the prediction related to the rebuilding of Jerusalem by Cyrus. A look at the prophecies of Isaiah will give us better insight into the value of biblical prophecy, both for ancient times and for us today.

ISAIAH

The name "Isaiah" derives from the Hebrew *Yesha'yahu* ("God is salvation"), and he is the prophet after whom the biblical Book of Isaiah is named. (Only some of the first thirty-nine chapters are attributed to him.) He was a significant contributor to Jewish and Christian traditions. His call to prophecy in about 742 B.C.E. coincided with the beginnings of the westward expansion of the Assyrian empire, which threatened Israel and which Isaiah proclaimed to be a warning from God to the godless.

The earliest recorded event in his life is his call to prophecy in the sixth chapter of the Book of Isaiah. The vision (probably in the Jerusalem Temple) that qualified him as a prophet is described in a first-person narrative. According to this account, he "saw" God and was overwhelmed by his contact with the divine glory and holiness. He became agonizingly aware of God's need for a messenger to the people of Israel, and, despite his own sense of inadequacy, he offered himself for God's service. He was thus commissioned to give voice to the divine word—no light undertaking. He was to condemn his own people and watch the nation crumble and perish. As he tells it, he was only too aware that, coming with such a message, he would experience bitter opposition, willful disbelief, and ridicule. His prophetic information came to him in the form of a vision and ended in a lifelong resolve to carry out his mission in spite of all difficulties.

ISAIAH'S PERSONAL HISTORY

At times the prophet's private life shows through the record as an aspect of his public message. Once when he went to confront a king, he took with him, to reinforce his prophetic word, a son with the symbolic name *Shear-yashuv* ("a remnant shall return"). Again, to memorialize a message, he sired a son from the "prophetess" (his wife) and saddled the child with his message as a name: *Maher-shalal-hash-baz* ("speed-spoil-hasten-plunder"), referring to the imminent spoliation by the Assyrians. Of Isaiah's parental home it is known only that his father's name was Amoz. Since he often spoke with kings, it is sometimes suggested that Isaiah was an aristocrat, possibly even of royal stock. Isaiah's sympathies, however, were emphatically with the victimized poor, not with the courtiers and wealthy. Some have said that he was of a priestly family, but his knowledge of cultic matters and the fact that his commissioning seemingly occurred in the Temple in Jerusalem are slender evidence for his priestly descent as against his unreserved condemnation of the priests and their domain: "I am fed up with roasting rams and the grease of fattened beasts," God proclaims in a famous passage in the first chapter.

Isaiah's experience bridges the classes and occupations. Whatever his family circumstances, in his youth he came to know poverty and the debauchery of the rich. He was at home with the unprotected, the widowed, and orphaned, with the dispossessed, homeless, landless, and with the resourceless victims of the moneyed man's court. He was also acquainted with the rapacious creators of the prevailing misery: self-centered lawmakers, venal judges, greedy land grabbers, thieves and wealthy drunkards, and irresponsible leaders, both civil and religious. In other words, he was intimately aware of the inequities and evils of human society.

HIS PROPHECY

The first chapters of the Book of Isaiah are an indictment of the Judeans for their abandonment of worship of God and their obsession with idolatry. But the main event in the lifetime of Isaiah is the loss of the "ten tribes" of Israel as a result of the rise of the Assyrian Empire, which plays a principal part in the prophecies of the first portion of the book. The most important contemporaneous events in Isaiah's imminent future are the piecemeal dissolution in three stages of the northern kingdom of Israel, and its complete annihilation as a state. Isaiah delivered his prophecies of the end of Israel to the house of David in Jerusalem and described the imminence of their loss in graphic terms. He said the spoil of the nation was to be completed in a matter of a few years from the birth of one of Isaiah's sons (Isa. 8:1–4).

After God has used these nations as his agents of punishment, Isaiah says they will disappear from the march of history, but Israel and Judah will be restored to fulfill God's purposes for them and have a continuing history. Isaiah first predicts this final great result in chapter two, that is, that the word of God will go out from Jerusalem and all nations will learn about the true God from the center of a restored Judah and Jerusalem (Isa. 2:2–3). Among his other prophecies, he intermingled messianic references that gave assurance that the whole house of Israel has a glorious future in spite of the horrors that Isaiah's generation experienced. This method continued until chapter forty, when he gave details of the physical restoration of the nation, during which time the Messiah would appear and establish Zion. In that section, the details are extraordinarily clear about the person and kingdom of the Messiah.

This much detail came from the inspiration of one mind, one heart, and all that is recorded as Isaiah's words has been seen to be fulfilled, as far as we can tell, exactly. Knowing this can inspire us to see what meaning these amazingly accurate predictions have for us.

BIBLICAL PROPHECY TODAY

The aspect of biblical prophecy that interests many of us today is prophecy as it relates to the End Time, and that is what we will be looking at in this book. What has been fulfilled, and what remains to be fulfilled? Are prophecies fulfilled only once, or do parts of them repeat until another part has been fulfilled? We will address these questions, as well as looking at a part of prophecy that tends to be forgotten. What is the meaning of the ethical and spiritual messages that were an integral part of every biblical prophecy? Every prophet brought a message from God about what humanity was to do. Does humanity have to follow God's directions before the promises of peace and prosperity are brought to fruition?

As we look to see how the biblical prophecies of Isaiah and others for the End Time apply to us in this time, however, we run into one major difficulty. Because so few people today know the Bible well, there has been a tendency for popular ideas to spring up about what the Bible actually says. The result has been fictionalized versions of End Time scenarios that confuse many aspects of real prophecy, such as confusing the battle of Armageddon and the final battle of Satan, and confusing the Apocalypse and the battle of Armageddon.

One example of this confusion is Hal Lindsey's 1970 book *The Late Great Planet Earth*. In that book, Lindsey assumed the Temple in Jerusalem would be rebuilt without describing the theological or scriptural basis for that theory. He also described the battle of Armageddon as the battle with Gog and Magog, without explaining that most scriptures describe that battle as a battle with "all nations," and that the Book of Revelation places the battle with Gog and Magog at the end of time, after the Millennium of peace. Lindsey did that because his theory that Gog referred to Russia wouldn't make sense if the battle of Gog was to happen over one thousand years in the future. To put forward his theory he had to leave out significant sections of the Bible.

A fictionalized version of prophecy has also been popularized in the *Left Behind* series of novels by Tim LaHaye and Jerry B. Jenkins. The assumptions in both *The Late Great Planet Earth* and the storyline of the *Left Behind* novels relate to a theological school called Dispensationalism.

DISPENSATIONALISM

Dispensationalism is very controversial among Christians, and a great debate rages on several counts. The Internet is full of arguments on both sides; the Dispensationalists imply that people who disagree with them will not be saved, and their opponents accuse them of everything from simple error to demonic delusion in the service of the Antichrist. A somewhat closer look at the basis of Dispensational belief may explain why this is such an emotional divide.

Dispensationalists believe that before the End Time there will occur what they call a Rapture of the Church, in which Jesus will spiritually come to take Christians, but not Jews, up to Heaven. In the *Left Behind* novels, only what they call born-again Christians are taken up in the Rapture. All those who are "left behind" at the Rapture must face the Tribulation, which Dispensationalists believe is a seven-year period during which the Antichrist will rise and take direct control of the earth, and during which most of the people on earth will die horrible and painful deaths. According to John Darby, one of the early proponents of Dispensational theology, only the Jews will live through the Tribulation. At the end of the seven-year period, Jesus will return in a physical form and will defeat Satan, convert the remaining Jews, and establish his rule on earth.

This theory is also called pretribulation or the pretrib theory. People who subscribe to this sometimes refer to themselves as "pretribbers." The name comes from the belief that Christians will be removed before the Tribulation, or pretrib. This group is set apart from those who believe that the taking up to Jesus of his people will happen after the Tribulation, or posttrib. These terms are essential for anyone doing an Internet search for these doctrines.

THE ORIGINS OF DISPENSATIONALISM

One of the first proponents of the idea of a separate Rapture of Christians was a fifteen-year-old, nineteenth-century Scottish girl named Margaret Macdonald, who was a member of the Catholic Apostolic Church. She had a vision of the return of the Messiah, which she wrote down and sent to various Christian leaders in Britain. Her description of the vision was later published. The first publication was in the book *Memoirs of James and George Macdonald, of Port Glasgow*, by Robert Norton (1840).

Margaret did not seem to expect a Rapture before the final Tribulation of the End Time. She saw the people of God being presented by one final test:

> *I saw the people of God in an awfully dangerous situation, surrounded by nets and entanglements, about to be tried, and many about to be deceived and fall. Now will the wicked be revealed, with all power and signs and lying wonders, so that it were possible the very elect will be deceived.*[1]

Her vision did contain the idea of a secret Rapture that not everyone could see, which is used by those who believe in a pretribulation Rapture of true Christians:

Only those who have the light of God within them will see the sign of his appearance. No need to follow them who say, see here, or see there, for his day shall be as the lightning to those in whom the living Christ is. 'Tis Christ in us that will lift us up—he is the light—'tis only those that are alive in him that will be caught up to meet him in the air.[2]

The extent to which Margaret Macdonald's vision influenced other proponents of the Rapture theory is a matter of dispute. Some give her credit for revealing the Rapture for the first time, while Christian opponents of the Rapture theory sometimes portray Margaret as a hysteric and delusional teenager. It is not surprising, therefore, that some proponents of the Rapture theory argue that the theory was passed down by learned Christian men.

John Darby, a nineteenth-century British evangelical minister, is usually credited with the creation of the Dispensational theories of the Rapture and End Time. The development of Dispensational belief is attributed to two small nineteenth-century groups, the Plymouth Brethren and the Millerites. The Plymouth Brethren were a group of British Christians who were dissatisfied with the Anglican Church. One of their largest churches was in Plymouth, England, where John Darby was invited to join the ministry. John Darby sometimes said that he was teaching "new truth," and sometimes that he was teaching "rediscovered truth." He wrote fairly extensively on his theories, and they became popular in Britain in the 1830s and in America in the 1850s.

The Millerites were followers of Williams Miller, who converted to Christianity in 1816. After a two-year study of the Bible, he began to teach that the Messiah would return in 1843 or 1844. Theories about the End Time were developed in expectation of that return.

Dispensational beliefs were popularized in the United States in the *Scofield Reference Bible*, published in 1909. Scofield taught that the Lord's Prayer is a Jewish prayer and should not be recited by Christians. The leading center for the study of Dispensationalist theology in the United States is the Dallas Theological Seminary, which was founded as a center of Dispensationalist theology in 1924. It has produced a Doctrinal Statement on Dispensationalism, which is widely accepted as the correct statement of the theology.

Dispensationalism in the United States is a subgroup of Fundamentalist Protestant Christianity. Fundamentalism is so called because it insists on the belief in five fundamentals of Christianity: (1) the literal truth of scripture; (2) the virgin birth and deity of Jesus; (3) that the death of Jesus atoned for the sins of humanity; (4) that the physical body of Jesus was resurrected; and (5) the imminent return of Jesus. Dispensationalists believe in these fundamentals but disagree on other issues that many believe are equally fundamental to Christian belief.

DISPENSATIONAL THEOLOGY

The controversy about Dispensational theology comes in the scriptural arguments the Dispensationalists use in support of their End Time scenario. They base the theory of the Rapture on several letters of Paul, as well as James, Peter, and John (1 Cor. 15:23; 1 Thess. 2:19, 3:13, 4:15, 5:23; 2 Thess. 2:1, 2:2; James 5:7; 2 Peter 1:16, 3:4; 1 John 2:28). These letters are all about the return of Jesus and the physical resurrection of bodies. Paul obviously expected that to happen during either his lifetime or the lifetimes of some of the people he was addressing. None of these letters says that there will be two returns of Jesus: one secret coming in a spiritual form to gather

Christians, and one coming in a physical form to rule the Millennium. Critics of Dispensationalists accuse them of adding to the scriptures or interpreting what isn't there.

The theory of the seven-year Tribulation that is intended for Jews and not for Christians is based primarily on Daniel 9:24–27:

> *Seventy weeks are determined upon thy people and upon thy holy city, to finish the transgression, and to make an end of sins, and to make reconciliation for iniquity, and to bring in everlasting righteousness, and to seal up the vision and prophecy, and to anoint the most Holy. Know therefore and understand, that from the going forth of the commandment to restore and to build Jerusalem unto the Messiah the Prince shall be seven weeks, and threescore and two weeks: the street shall be built again, and the wall, even in troublous times. And after threescore and two weeks shall Messiah be cut off, but not for himself: and the people of the prince that shall come shall destroy the city and the sanctuary; and the end thereof shall be with a flood, and unto the end of the war desolations are determined. And he shall confirm the covenant with many for one week: and in the midst of the week he shall cause the sacrifice and the oblation to cease, and for the overspreading of abominations he shall make it desolate, even until the consummation, and that determined shall be poured upon the desolate.*

Most Christians agree that this prediction is really referring to seventy weeks of years, instead of seventy years. We will discuss this more fully later. Exactly how many years this time period consists of is a matter of theological debate, depending on whether a lunar or solar year is used and on other factors.

Without going into those details, one of the most popular traditional interpretations of this prophecy has been that the Jewish people would be freed from the Babylonian slavery they were experiencing at the time of the prophecy and would return to Jerusalem to rebuild the Temple that the Babylonians had destroyed. At the end of the time period, the Messiah would come for the first time but would be cut off (killed). The time period between Ezra's return to Jerusalem in 458 B.C.E., when a second Temple was in fact built, and the tentative date of Jesus' baptism in 26 C.E., was 483 years, or sixty-nine weeks of years. In the last of the seventy weeks of years, Jesus conducted his ministry and was crucified, or cut off. After his death, the Temple was destroyed.

Another interpretation popular among modern scholars and theologians is that this prophecy refers to the defilement of the Temple by Antiochus Epiphanes in about 189 B.C.E. (see chapter 10). Antiochus Epiphanes was an invading prince who defiled the Temple for three and a half years, a half of a week of years.

Both of these interpretations are based on the belief that the prophecy of Daniel 9:24–27 has already been fulfilled. Dispensationalists argue that these verses are about future prophecy and refer only to Jews. The Jews must complete a final seven years of tribulation to be purified just before the Messiah comes to rule the Millennium. One Dispensationalist website explains it like this: "Daniel's seventieth week specifically refers to the purging of the nation Israel, and not the Church. These were the clear words spoken to Daniel. The church doesn't need purging from sin. It is already clean."[3]

The idea that Jews need to be purged from sin by a horrible time of tribulation and pain, while Christians do not, is understandably controversial. The explanation for this difference in treatment is where Dispensationalism gets its name. They believe in three dispensations or, to put it simply, time periods. There was the time of the Law, which was before Jesus, the time of Grace, which was after Jesus and includes the present, and there will be the time of the Millennium. There were different ways of salvation in the first two dispensations. Christianity has not replaced Judaism in this theory but has just taken center stage, so to speak.

Dispensationalists see a clear distinction between God's program for Israel and God's program for the Church. God is not finished with Israel. The Church didn't take Israel's place. Jews have been set aside temporarily, but in the End Times will be brought back to the promised land, cleansed, and given a new heart (Gen. 12; Deut. 30; 2 Sam. 7; Jer. 31).[4]

Therefore, Dispensationalists argue that some parts of the Bible are meant for Jews only, and some parts are meant for Christians. This is not as simple as dividing the Old and New Testaments, because Dispensationalists argue that some of the statements of Jesus are also meant only for Jews. This leads some to highly controversial conclusions, e.g., the Ten Commandments, as part of the Law, are only for Jews, and that the Lord's Prayer, even though given by Jesus, is only for Jews, because it speaks of a kingdom yet to come.

This division of the Bible raises one of the most hotly disputed issues: the interpretation of Matthew 24:1–30:

> *And Jesus went out, and departed from the temple: and his disciples came to him for to shew him the buildings of the temple. And Jesus said unto them, See ye not all these things? verily I say unto you, There shall not be left here one stone upon another, that shall not be thrown down.*
>
> *And as he sat upon the mount of Olives, the disciples came unto him privately, saying, Tell us, when shall these things be? and what shall be the sign of thy coming, and of the end of the world? And Jesus answered and said unto them, Take heed*

that no man deceive you. For many shall come in my name, saying, I am Christ; and shall deceive many. And ye shall hear of wars and rumors of wars: see that ye be not troubled: for all these things must come to pass, but the end is not yet. For nation shall rise against nation, and kingdom against kingdom: and there shall be famines, and pestilences, and earthquakes, in divers places. All these are the beginning of sorrows.

Then shall they deliver you up to be afflicted, and shall kill you: and ye shall be hated of all nations for my name's sake. And then shall many be offended, and shall betray one another, and shall hate one another. And many false prophets shall rise, and shall deceive many. And because iniquity shall abound, the love of many shall wax cold. But he that shall endure unto the end, the same shall be saved. And this gospel of the kingdom shall be preached in all the world for a witness unto all nations; and then shall the end come.

When ye therefore shall see the abomination of desolation, spoken of by Daniel the prophet, stand in the holy place (whoso readeth, let him understand). Then let them which be in Judaea flee into the mountains: Let him which is on the housetop not come down to take any thing out of his house: Neither let him which is in the field return back to take his clothes. And woe unto them that are with child, and to them that give suck in those days! But pray ye that your flight be not in the winter, neither on the sabbath day: For then shall be great tribulation, such as was not since the beginning of the world to this time, no, nor ever shall be. And except those days should be shortened, there should no flesh be saved: but for the elect's sake those days shall be shortened. Then if any man shall say unto you, Lo, here is Christ, or there; believe it not.

For there shall arise false Christs, and false prophets, and shall shew great signs and wonders; insomuch that, if it were possible, they shall deceive the very elect. Behold, I have told you before. Wherefore if they shall say unto you, Behold, he is in the desert; go not forth: behold, he is in the secret chambers; believe it not. For as the lightning cometh out of the east, and shineth even unto the west; so shall also the coming of the Son of man be. For wheresoever the carcass is, there will the eagles be gathered together.

Immediately after the tribulation of those days shall the sun be darkened, and the moon shall not give her light, and the stars shall fall from heaven, and the powers of the heavens shall be shaken: And then shall appear the sign of the Son of man in heaven: and then shall all the tribes of the earth mourn, and they shall see the Son of man coming in the clouds of heaven with power and great glory.

Dispensationalists take the reference of Jesus to Daniel to mean that the prophecy of Daniel will be fulfilled in the End Time. They also take the warning of persecution and suffering to be aimed at Jews only, or at non-Christians. They argue this even though Jesus is talking to his disciples and saying "you."

Critics say that Dispensationalists are showing their unwillingness to suffer as Christ suffered and as he asked his people to endure. They say that by arguing that Jesus wasn't really referring to Christians when he spoke to his disciples, Dispensationalists are criticizing or revising the teachings of Jesus.

The most common modern interpretation of Matthew 24 is that Jesus was predicting that the second Temple would be destroyed and that the Jews would be killed and driven out of Israel. We know that this actually happened less than half a century later, but no one else was predicting such a thing. First-century Christians also believed that the End Time would happen in their lifetimes and seemed to understand the predictions of Matthew 24 as meaning that the destruction of the Temple and the return of Jesus would happen at the same time. Since the amazing prediction of Jesus that the Temple would be destroyed and the people of Israel dispersed actually happened, and the End Time did not occur at the same time, subsequent Christians have mostly assumed that Jesus was giving predictions for two different times: 70 C.E. and the End Time. This interpretation is consistent with the Book of Revelation.

Dispensationalists and others argue that both the destruction of the Temple and the End Time will happen at the same time, so that the Temple must be rebuilt a third time before the final End Time and the return of Jesus can occur. We will discuss this at more length in chapter 10.

The last really controversial belief of the Dispensationalists is the assumption that Satan, not God, is the ruler of our world. According to the generally accepted doctrinal statement put out by the Dallas Theological Seminary, "We believe that Satan was judged at the Cross, though not then executed, and that he, a usurper, now rules as the 'god of this world.' "[5] This leads to the assumption that religious traditions that disagree with them are demonic in origin:

We believe that Satan is the originator of sin, and that, under the permission of God, he, through subtlety, led our first parents into transgression, thereby accomplishing their moral fall and subjecting them and their posterity to his own power; that he is the enemy of God and the people of God, opposing and exalting himself above all that is called God or that is worshiped; and that he who in the beginning said, "I will be like the most High," in his warfare appears as an angel of light, even counterfeiting the works of God by fostering religious movements and systems of doctrine, which systems in every case are characterized by a denial of the efficacy of the blood of Christ and of salvation by grace alone (Gen. 3:1–19; Rom. 5:12–14; 2 Cor. 4:3–4, 11:13–15; Eph. 6:10–12; 2 Thess. 2:4; 1 Tim. 4:1–3).[6]

Those who disagree with the idea that Satan rules the world are often outraged at the suggestion that Satan is capable of usurping power or that God could be defeated in that way.

Dispensationalist and other similar interpretation of biblical texts are based on what they call literal interpretations of the Bible. We will see, however, that these are usually literal interpretations from an eighteenth- to twenty-first-century point of view or worldview. There is very little, if any, attempt to determine what the ancient writers literally intended to convey. Dispensationalists oppose others who interpret biblical texts in metaphorical or symbolic ways. Some people do not believe in a literal Millennium, for example, but believe that the Millennium refers to a spiritual or symbolic time since the first coming of Jesus.

In this book we will assume that in many cases biblical writers were referring to real and not metaphorical or symbolic events, though we will keep in mind that real events were often described symbolically in ancient times. This makes interpretation of the prophecy very challenging. On the other hand, our "literal" interpretation will be based on the information we have as to how ancient people communicated. We will look for what they intended to say instead of what their words sound like to a modern consciousness operating from a worldview very different from the ancient world.

We will use the Book of Revelation as our map of events, though we will discuss both Old and New Testament prophecies, as well as other related prophecies. The Book of Revelation predicts the rise of two "Beasts," an Apocalypse consisting of a series of tragic events, a battle of Armageddon, a spiritual awakening of an unnumbered multitude, the return of the Messiah, and a Millennium of peace.

CHAPTER 2

ASTROLOGY AND MYTH
IN THE BIBLE

M odern people disagree on many cultural, economic, and religious issues, but we still share a basic world-view. For example, people of modern times tend to think the earth is round and that it is one of several planets orbiting the sun. We usually don't think the sun is a god, as many ancients did. We share a worldview that has a lot to do with the discoveries of science in the last centuries.

In antiquity, people also shared a basic worldview. The different groups, such as Jews, Pagans, and Christians, had significant differences, but in many essential ways they were more like each other than any of their modern-day counterparts. They lived closer to the earth and the seasons than we do, and they perceived influences that we rarely think of. They felt the influence of the planets, of numbers, and of the effects of harmony and disharmony. They disagreed about monotheism and the relative powerfulness of their gods, but they didn't disagree about the effects of the planets, of form, and of number. They understood those things to influence their lives in ways we can only imagine. They believed that the interaction of form and number was the *way* God worked in the world.

They believed that if they could understand the meaning of things like form, number, and harmony, they could understand the will of God. So if we want to understand the writings of these ancient people, we have to look at them from the perspective of the ancient worldview.

MYTH

Part of this shared perspective was the importance of myth. Understanding of myth was very important in Greek culture, for example. Truths that could not be directly transmitted by speech could be communicated through myth and symbol, but the understanding of them depended on the development of the listener/reader. As the writer David Fideler writes:

> *Platonists stressed the fact that reality is hierarchical, consisting of different levels. Mythology, it was held, refers to many levels of reality simultaneously. Therefore, if we are to gain insight into the nature of the gods—the divine principles that underlie creation—a particularly instructive approach involves the philosophical interpretation of myth.[1]*

People in antiquity freely borrowed from each other's myths in much the same way we do today. If we want to describe someone who is obsessed by his or her own looks, we might call the person narcissistic. This is a reference to the Greek myth of Narcissus, who used to spend hours gazing at himself in the water. We don't use this reference because we actually believe in the myth, nor do we intend to imply that the vain person really is Narcissus. We use the term because we know it carries a lot of meaning to our listeners. The ancients did the same thing. As Fideler puts it:

> *Certain philosophic schools, especially the Platonists and Stoics, drew upon traditional myths to illustrate insights that transcend merely logical description. Moreover, many held that the interpretations of the traditional myths, like the pursuit of philosophy itself, constituted, at its core, a process of initiation.*[2]

There is an unfortunate tendency among some biblical interpreters to interpret myths as though they are literally true. Whenever we see a version of an old myth or of a story from an old scripture, this should be a clue to us that this point is probably not meant to be taken literally. In antiquity, innovation was not only frowned on, it was considered heresy. No one would claim to be teaching something new. It was essential to tie any teaching to tradition, and constant references to well-known myth and accepted scripture was the most common way to do that.

ASTROLOGY

Astrology, as we know it in the West, has been traced back to Mesopotamia, with the earliest texts dated before 1600 B.C.E. Some scholars believe that the Mesopotamians came up with the concept of the circle and the division into twelve signs. Between 640 and 560, Mesopotamian astrologers brought the system into Greece. There is also a Greek record of a later visitor who was widely recognized for his contribution. The Mesopotamian scholar Berossos, priest of Bel, moved to Greece and wrote a treatise on astrology called *Babyloniaca* in about 281. The people of Greece were so grateful for this information that they put up a statue of Berossos in Athens. Some scholars believe that the Greeks, not the Mesopotamians, were the first to put the zodiac in a circle.[3]

Astrology spread throughout the ancient world. It appears, for example, in the Qumran documents,[4] which have been dated to the time between 200 B.C.E. and 70 C.E., most of them in the earlier time. Astrology has also been found in the Babylonian Talmud.[5]

Talmud is the Hebrew word for learning or study. It became the name for a collection of discussions and debates among rabbis. During a period stretching from mid–first century to the third century, the Jewish Law was written down. Up until that time the law had been passed on in a purely oral form and memorized by the keepers of the law. Sometime before his death in 217 C.E., Rabbi Judah ben Simeon, who is known as Rabbi Judah the Prince, collected the various texts of the Law and composed one uniform text. It was call the "Mishna," from the Hebrew word *ShNH*, to repeat or memorize. For several hundred years after that, the unified text continued to be passed on in oral as well as written form.

Rabbis commented on the Mishna, and in about 400 C.E. rabbis in Palestine collected the Mishna and commentaries into one text, which was called the Palestinian Talmud. About a century later, rabbis in Babylon compiled a Talmud, including the Gemara of Abba Arika, called *Rab*, the Master. The Babylonian Talmud was much more extensive than the Palestinian and came to be more authoritative.

This rabbinic writing had several astrological references. For example, the commentary *Pesikta Rabbati* tells us that the planets and signs of the zodiac were among God's first creations. The Babylonian Talmud tractate *Shabbat* contains a number of related stories illustrating the rabbinic attitudes toward astrology. In the first story, Rabbi Judah the Prince claims that it is the day of the week that determines one's personality, while in the next story Rabbi Hanina Bar Hama says, "Not the constellation of the day but that of the hour is the determining influence." In the third story, Rabbi Hanina Bar Hama from Palestine and Rabbi Johanan Bar Nappaha from Mesopotamia debate whether astrology affected the Jews. The fourth story relates how God changed Abraham's horoscope so that he might beget Isaac.

ASTROLOGICAL SYMBOLISM

As a preliminary backdrop to the coming prophecies, we can take a brief look at some of the astrological symbolism present in the Bible, if only to give us a sense of one of the methods used to encode the prophetic message of the book. But it should be made clear from the outset that we are not using astrology in the sense of the horoscopes that appear in newspapers and magazines and assert that one-twelfth of the entire world population will all be behaving in the same way at the same time! Astrology is more subtle and complex than that.

Let us look at a quotation from the Book of Revelation:

> *After this I looked, and behold, a door was opened in heaven: and the first voice which I heard was as it were of a trumpet talking with me; which said, Come up hither, and I will shew thee things which must be hereafter. . . . And before the throne there was a sea of glass like unto crystal, and in the midst of the throne, and round about the throne, were four beasts full*

of eyes before and behind, And the first beast was like a lion, and the second beast like a calf, and the third beast had a face as a man, and the fourth beast was like a flying eagle. And the four beasts had each of them six wings about him; and they were full of eyes within, and they rest not day and night, saying, Holy, holy, holy, Lord God Almighty, which was, and is, and is to come (Rev. 4:1–8).

The "four beasts" mentioned in this chapter of Revelation—the Calf (Ox), the Lion, the Eagle, and the Man—relate to the four main zodiacal signs of Taurus, Leo, Scorpio (the eagle), and Aquarius (the human water bearer). Revelation is not the only book in the Bible in which the same four beasts are mentioned. In the Old Testament Book of Ezekiel, the prophet Ezekiel, for example, relates a vision in which scenes appeared to him including a Man, a Lion, an Ox, and an Eagle.

The man symbol is accepted throughout astrology as the Water Bearer of Aquarius, the lion as Leo, the calf or ox obviously indicates the sign of Taurus, and the eagle signifies the higher values of Scorpio, though this is perhaps less well known except among astrologers. The scorpion symbol is the lower psychic expression of the sign of Scorpio, while the eagle is the higher.

Esoteric scholar Manly P. I. Hall, in his classic book *The Secret Teachings of All Ages,* tells us:

Probably the rarest form of Scorpio is that of an Eagle. The arrangement of the stars of the constellation bears as much resemblance to a flying bird as to a scorpion. Scorpio, being the sign of occult initiation, the flying eagle—the king of the birds—represents the highest and most spiritual type of Scorpio, in which it transcends the venomous insect of the earth.[6]

It is entirely appropriate that within the Bible the more rare forms of astrological symbolism would be used.

These same four symbols also appeared in Egyptian and Babylonian traditions of wisdom, specifically at the entrance to the Great Pyramid of Giza. The archetypical Sphinx is composed of the head of a man, the body of a bull, the claws of a lion, and the wings of an eagle. The Bible, as a part of the Jewish and Christian traditions, integrated these symbols from the distant past and used them to form part of the basis for its prophetic substance. Although astrology is not the primary interpretative force behind the Bible, within the first four chapters of Revelation we see the scene set by reference to astrological symbols.

Christianity later attempted to reduce the significance of astrology by emphasizing its occult, heretical nature. Astrology was concerned with "the heavens," the domain of God, and was therefore forbidden to man, but in the symbolism of the Bible, astrology is so clearly present that it has survived through Christianity to remain significant in our interpretations of the predictions.

THE PISCEAN AND AQUARIAN AGES

Part of the study of astrology is based on grand periods of movement of the heavens. These last around two thousand years or so and, strangely enough, move backwards through the astrological star signs. These grand time scales greatly influence the ages of earth and its people.

The age of Aries ran from around 2000 B.C.E. to the time of the birth of Christ. Cusp periods last about 100 years, so the cusp of Aries and Pisces ran from approximately 50 B.C.E. to 50 C.E., a time period that included the entire life of Jesus and the beginning of

Christianity. About fifty years ago, around 1950, we entered into the cusp between the Age of Pisces and the Age of Aquarius. The cusp period will end in about 2050, and the full effect of the Aquarian Age will be felt. A cusp period is a time when the energies of the new age begin to emerge but the influence of the old age is still in effect, so it is a transition period. Since we often resist new ways of being, times of change can be difficult for us.

Aries, a fire sign, represents the fire of ignition, of initial creation, of the beginning of the zodiac itself, and, as such, drove many cultures and civilizations forward. A form of tribal thought and law began in the Arian age, which superseded the more primitive tribalism of the preceding age of Taurus. During the Age of Aries, there was a tendency to try and dominate the natural environment and to develop ideas of fairness and laws to enforce them.

The Piscean Age broke away from the tribal perspective, and humanity began to develop a clearer sense of individuality and of self. Laws began to protect the rights of individuals, a concept unheard of in earlier times. These rights were codified in documents like the Magna Carta, the United States Constitution, and United Nations declarations on human rights. They are now so widely codified in the laws of various countries that we have a tendency to forget that the idea of individual rights is a very modern one.

Pisces also inclines toward a dualistic perspective, so that we tend to focus on either/or. During the Piscean Age, we have thought in terms of East and West, Church and State, body and spirit, male and female, good and evil, and political views of the right and left. The world is seen in terms of opposing opposites that cannot be resolved or harmonized.

As we enter the age of Aquarius at the beginning of the twenty-first century, we are moving from an astrological age identified by fish to one represented by a human figure, the water carrier. In this age, we will move from either/or to a search for an inclusive unity. The religions of the world have begun to try to understand each other in ways never thought of before, and we are thinking globally. We speak of the global marketplace and global technology.

Each astrological age helps humanity develop its consciousness in new ways. It is important for us to understand how each age affects us and be prepared to let go of what is no longer helpful. Each age has its way of doing things. In this time of major transition to the Aquarian Age, it is becoming less and less effective to operate in the way of the Piscean Age, as the cusp progresses. The Age of Pisces has ended, and we are in the beginning of the Aquarian Age, in which only a remnant of Piscean influence remains. This is the time to understand what the Aquarian Age is and how it will affect us, since its influence is ever increasing. We cannot understand prophecy and expectations for the Age of Aquarius based on our experiences of the Piscean Age.

There are broad astrological influences of the sign of Aquarius in our time. Any prophet with astrological knowledge writing during the previous grand time period—that of the Piscean or Arian Age, would have known that Saturn would dominate the Aquarian Age. This would have indicated to prophets that the end of the twentieth century and the beginning of the twenty-first century was to be a time of penetrating, scientific, and philosophical reason that would prompt questions rather than acceptance. Saturn also implies the need for control, the structuring of natural resources, and an intelligent use of the world's resources to make the present more sustainable. In mythology, Saturn was the god of agriculture and presided over the golden age and the laws of good farming and conservation of the earth.

The Piscean Age, which very much influenced the early Christian era, was one of unquestioning religious faith, of a belief in miracles and magic as the very foundation of life. This gave birth to modern belief in God's indisputable presence—a belief that has dominated modern history until now. It was in this climate that we saw the rise of Christianity, the Roman Catholic Church, Mahayana Buddhism, modern Hinduism, and Islam.

The Aquarian Age, by contrast, will eventually bring us out of this miraculous, unquestioned approach to life, into a time when nothing goes uncontested and science delves into all matters and asks the most piercing questions. Philosophy and reason pluck the petals from every rose and dissect every cell of existence. Each process of discovery is a process of movement—a verb rather than a noun. In the fifty years of the Aquarian cusp period, we have already witnessed this.

The domination of Saturn also gives rise to a certain kind of political revolution, for in the area of social leadership there is also the constant process of questioning. We have seen already in the last half of the twentieth century that political revolution has changed. We saw the war in Vietnam and the controversy surrounding it, the fall of communism in much of the world, and unrest in parts of the former USSR.

Another important characteristic of the Aquarian period of life is that of the collective. There is, and will continue to be, a growth pattern through collective activity rather than individual. Countries move together into continents, or states into nations. In the last fifty years we have seen alliances among Middle Eastern nations and the formation of the European Union. These are perfect examples of the Aquarian tendency toward group activity. The ecological movement presently filling the media is another example of the same tendency, and the Gaia movement—the whole-earth movement, the concept of a global community—is characteristic of an Aquarian influence.

But we may ask, if everything is supposed to be scientific and reasonable, why is there so much chaos around right now? When we look at the biblical prophecies written during the Arian and Piscean ages, we will see that the majority of the predictions that relate to our own age are concerned with the chaos and devastation we are now experiencing—the wars and terrors that much of the world witnesses on a daily basis. Why does such a rational age suffer even more than any prior to it?

The answer is, first, that Aquarius is not only the sign of reason and science but also the sign in which humanity is attempting to master the instinctual world of nature. There are bound to be many scientific breakthroughs that result in radical changes in knowledge and lifestyle. Second, we are now in the cusp of the two signs, coming toward Aquarius. This cusp between Pisces and Aquarius has already lasted more than half a century and will continue for a further half century. These grand astrological changes do not happen suddenly but slowly. Everything is in flux because we are altering our perception toward an age of change, but it is also in flux because such massive changes create anxiety.

As human consciousness begins to manifest the characteristics of the Aquarian Age, it also has to deal with the anxieties that such transformation evokes. We are on a cusp of change. The definitions of reality have slipped—Church, State, family—and the new definitions have not yet established themselves. Everything in society as a whole seems to be in a mess, because we are trying to readjust to the new "rules"—rules that demand faith. And these questions will inevitably lead to answers that will eventually bring some peace of mind. But for the moment, that peace of mind is still only a dim light at the end of the tunnel.

And the more powerful the changes, the more likely we are to try to withdraw from them. The establishment of the European Union is a perfect example of this. As the tendency grows toward joining together into larger nations and groups of nations, so the tribal instinct comes to the surface to maintain the small groups. We fight to hold on to our national heritages, languages, traditions, even currencies, as these disappear into larger concepts and structures. We are, perhaps, afraid that the huge collective will stifle the expression and needs of the individual. There have been many empires that have crushed the people that made them, only to collapse into disaster. There are no easy answers to the future. We are groping in the dark for new solutions—the perfect scenario of the Aquarian Age.

These Aquarian characteristics and their interaction on the cusp between Pisces and Aquarius would also have been evident to the biblical prophets that comprehended astrology. Knowledge of these characteristics might, in fact, have led the prophets to form many of these prophecies.

CHAPTER 3

THE SECRET OF NUMBERS
IN THE BIBLE

GEMATRIA

The word "gematria" comes from the Greek word *geometria*, or geometry. The gematria was a system of interpreting the meaning of the numerical equivalents of words, and those meanings were found in a complex mathematical system. Some modern interpreters describe it as a system to give numerical value to words, but that isn't quite correct. Ancient languages, such as Hebrew, Greek, and Latin, had no separate numeral system, such as the Arabic numerals we use today. They used the letters of the alphabet as both letters and numbers. So the letters of those alphabets not only symbolically but literally had two meanings. Every word had an obvious numerical value that anyone who knew the alphabet could calculate. Not everyone, however, knew how to interpret the meaning of those numbers.

A CHRISTIAN SYSTEM

The gematria was so widespread during the early years of Christianity that it was mentioned by several of the early Church Fathers:

Irenaeus, Hippolytus, Tertullian, and Jerome. These Church Fathers sometimes referred to the use of gematria by other Christian writers. The gematria eventually came to be associated with the Gnostics (astrology was probably associated with them as well), and in the great split between Gnostics and orthodox during the second century, the gematria came to be ignored in orthodox Christianity.

The sum of the numbers represented by the letters of the word was the number of the word, and from the standpoint of gematria two words were equivalent if they added up to the same number. Not only was gematria used from the earliest days for the interpretation of Bible passages, but there are indications that the writers of the Bible had practiced the art. Thus Abraham, proceeding to rescue his brother Elisasar, drives forth 318 slaves. Is it just a coincidence that the Hebrew word Eliasar adds up to 318?[1]

ORTHODOX AND GNOSTIC DISPUTE

Gnosticism is a broad term that has been used to describe a wide range of beliefs, so it is hard to give an accurate definition that would fit all the examples. Generally, Gnostics tended to make strict divisions between the physical world and the spiritual, and Gnostics tended to value internal experience over external doctrine. Orthodox Christianity was so successful in destroying Gnosticism that until a few decades ago we knew about it primarily from the polemics written by its opponents, which, of course, tended to exaggerate and give only one side. In 1945, a library of texts was discovered at Nag Hammadi in Egypt, which has come to be known as the Gnostic Gospels. It took thirty years for these texts to be translated and revealed to the world, because most scholars were refused access to them. When they were finally available, the diversity of the Nag Hammadi material made it clear that early Christianity was not a homogeneous and unified group, but a rich and varied collection of people with different points of view and understandings of Jesus and Christian practice. The Gnostic Gospels portray Jesus and his mission in a way very different from the Gospels that became the New Testament years later.

Orthodox Christianity claimed that the dispute with the Gnostics concerned the physical nature of Jesus. While that was, no doubt, an issue with some groups, the real dispute was the authority of the Church. Orthodox Christianity held that the Church had the sole right to interpret scripture and to create doctrine and that the Church hierarchy of deacons, priests, and bishops had the right to control the Church. The Gnostics believed that authentic spiritual experience was the only true authority, and that the Church hierarchy and doctrine did not apply to someone who *knew* from his or her own experience. The insistence of the Roman Catholic Church that it had the sole right to interpret scripture became an issue in the Protestant Reformation in Europe many centuries later.

After nineteen hundred years of orthodox Christianity, we tend to think of astrology and the gematria as being non-Christian, but that wasn't the case in the first century when John was writing the Book of Revelation or when the Old Testament prophecies were written. Many people have misinterpreted biblical prophecy because they have tried to understand it from the perspective of orthodox European Christianity, which had lost touch with some aspects of ancient thought.

Many ancient Greek Church documents ended with the number 99 (ΦΘ). The numerical value for amen (AMHN) is 99. So the number 99 was used to mean amen. This shows that basic gematria was in widespread use in early Christianity.

In Galatians 3:17, Paul writes that the Mosaic Law came four hundred and thirty years after God's covenant with Abraham. That makes no sense in terms of calendar years, but the numerical value for the word "law" in Greek (NOMOΣ) is 430, so it is very likely that Paul knew Greek gematria, which is not surprising, since we know he received a Greek education.

In an early Christian writing that was not placed in the canon, the Epistle of Barnabas, it is said that the story of Moses circumcising 318 men in the Hebrew Bible was an anticipation of Jesus on the cross. The cross is symbolized by the Greek letter Tau (T), which has a numerical value of 300. The first two letters of Jesus in Greek (IH) have a numerical value of 18. So Jesus on the cross was 318. The number 318 is also the numerical value of Helios, a Greek name for the sun. Because Jesus was said to be the light of the world, this may have linked the number 318 to Jesus in early Christian interpretations.[2]

It is clear that the gematria was used in early Christian thought and writing, and it would be fairly unthinkable that John, who we are told lived on Patmos in the heart of Greek culture, failed to use it. We know he did use it in calculating the number 666, so we need to keep the gematria in mind when we look at the text of Revelation.

The gematria not only produced the numerical equivalent of words, but it allowed words with the same numerical value to be associated with each other. Tobias Dantzig, a professor of mathematics at the University of Maryland, has described the process.

The second-century Church leader Irenaeus was familiar with the gematria and knew how to use it. He was born somewhere in Asia and eventually became the bishop of Lyons after the previous incumbent was martyred. He is best known for his writings against Gnosticism, which he considered heresy. He was declared a saint by the Roman Catholic Church.

The second-century writer Tertullian also showed a familiarity with these teachings. He is best known for his writings against the teachings he considered to be heresy. He later left the Church to join a splinter group and then to form a group of his own. Because Tertullian died outside the Church, he was not considered a saint, but his writings on heresy make him a leading figure among the Church Fathers.

In the third century Hippolytus of Rome demonstrated that he knew the gematria. Hippolytus was a controversial figure who became involved in a dispute with the elected pope on the issue of the relationship between the Father and Son in the Holy Trinity. He was reconciled with the pope shortly before his death, and was later declared a saint by the Roman Catholic Church.

Two of the Church's best-known teachers and writers lived at the end of the fourth and beginning of the fifth centuries. They both displayed a knowledge of gematria as a way of understanding Christian teaching. Jerome is best known for his translation of the Bible from Greek to Latin in a version known as the Vulgate. The Vulgate is still considered the official Bible of the Roman Catholic Church. Jerome also wrote extensive biblical commentaries. He has been declared both a saint and a Doctor, or revered teacher, of the Roman Catholic Church.

Jerome's contemporary, Augustine of Hippo, has been one of the most influential thinkers in Western Christianity. He was born in Africa to a pagan father and Christian mother, but eventually became the Bishop of Hippo. He, too, has been declared both a saint and a Doctor of the Roman Catholic Church.

These Church leaders and Catholic saints lived and worked from the second to fifth centuries and were all familiar with gematria and its role in understanding the Bible. On this evidence, it is clear that the gematria was a system that Christians shared with many others in the early days of Christianity. Since these early Church leaders believed the gematria was relevant in understanding the Bible and Christian teaching, it is evident that it will be worthwhile for us to pay attention to it as well.

UNITY AND HARMONY

The study of the gematria involved Pythagorean ideas about mathematics and geometry. Pythagoras of Samos was the son of Mnesarchus of Tyre, a city on the Mediterranean coast of Syria, and Pythais of Samos, an island off the coast of modern-day Turkey. He spent his childhood in Tyre, but is said to have traveled widely with his father and to have studied with Chaldeans in Tyre. He went to Egypt to study in 535 B.C.E., when Samos was taken over by a tyrant. He may have studied geometry with the Egyptians, or he may have studied it with his earlier teachers. Pythagoras accepted many of the practices of the Egyptian priests, such as their secrecy, their refusal to eat beans, and their refusal to wear animal skins.

Egypt was invaded while Pythagoras was there, and he was captured and taken prisoner to Babylon, where he studied arithmetic, music, and other mathematical sciences with the priests or Magi. He left in about 520 B.C.E. and returned to Samos. Shortly after his return, he went to Crete to study Greek law and then came back to Samos to found a school.

Apparently Pythagoras was not well received in Samos, so in 518 B.C.E. he moved his school to southern Italy. The school was divided into levels. The closest disciples lived with Pythagoras as vegetarians and had no personal possessions. Others lived normal lives in the surrounding community. The school was open to both men and women, an unusual approach in that time. In 508, the school in Italy was attacked by opponents. Some reports say Pythagoras was killed in the attack, other sources say that he escaped to Metapontium, in Greece, where he lived the rest of his life, while still others say that he returned to Italy. We do know that his school continued to thrive for many years.

The key tenets of the Pythagorean school were that:

1. at its deepest level, reality is mathematical in nature,

2. philosophy can be used for spiritual purification,

3. the soul can rise to union with the divine,

4. certain symbols have a mystical significance, and

5. all brothers of the order should observe strict loyalty and secrecy.

The underlying principle was that the One, the unity, pervades the many or the multiplicity. This is usually called the doctrine of Emanations, but Pythagoras called it the Science of Numbers. He taught his close disciples that this science had been handed down by divine instructors of the Third Race, and first taught to the Greeks by Orpheus and passed down in secrecy to a select few. Pythagoras learned these mysteries just before they began to degenerate. Pythagoras believed that the study of philosophy activated what he called the eye of wisdom, but is now called the pineal gland. This is the same organ many Eastern traditions call the third eye and believe is activated by meditation.

For Pythagoras there is a unity that lies beyond all manifestation in the physical world, and this unity has no number. The geometrical figure closest to this state of nothingness was the zero or circle. The first number was one, which was a divine number. This was the apex of the equilateral triangle of Father, Mother, and Son. Because of this, the letter Delta, Δ, was used to refer to the One. This is still used in our word "deity."

The cross or square of four symbolized the natural world, while the pentacle or five-pointed star symbolized the human, with four limbs and the fifth human principle of Manas, or conscious thought. The number six was associated with the star formed by overlapping triangles, the same symbol now used for Judaism. It symbolized the union of spirit and matter, as well as sexual union. Seven was the Pythagorean perfect number, since it was a combination of the divine triangle of the Father, Mother, and Son, and the square or cross of the natural world. This was sometimes applied to the human, with the triangle representing the higher, unchanging, spiritual aspects, and the square symbolizing the ever-changing physical reality.

Ten was the number that brought the others back to unity. This was symbolized in the Tetraktys:

$$\bullet$$
$$\bullet \quad \bullet$$
$$\bullet \quad \bullet \quad \bullet$$
$$\bullet \quad \bullet \quad \bullet \quad \bullet$$

This is an arrangement of ten dots in the form of a triangle. The top three dots symbolize the invisible and metaphysical world, and the lower seven symbolize the realm of physical phenomena.

The geometrical forms of the circle, triangle, and square are found in nature and so were taken to be symbols of the eternal realm that exists beyond matter. David Fideler, an expert on ancient cosmology, writes:

> *The Babylonians and Egyptians as well as the Greeks studied geometry mathematics in antiquity. In Greek philosophy, it was said that universal Forms are the structures that underlie the Cosmos. Plato said that "geometry is the knowledge of the eternally existent."*[3]

In the *Republic*, Plato suggested that philosophers study the Pythagorean sciences of arithmetic, geometry, harmonics (musical tuning theory), and astronomy. The Pythagoreans believed that these essential areas of study had unique relationships to number: Arithmetic was the study of number in itself; Geometry was the study of number in space. Harmonics was the study of number in time, and Astronomy (or Cosmology) was the study of number in space and time.[4]

Pythagoras was the first of the ancient Greeks to call himself a philosopher, which means a lover of wisdom. He taught that things are arranged and defined by Number. The Number represents the working of the divine sphere, which makes Number a blueprint of creation.

In these calculations, the square roots of 2 and 3 underlie the genesis of form in the actual world. Formative principles expressed by 1, $\sqrt{2}$, $\sqrt{3}$ are what brings the visible Universe into existence:

$600 \times 1 = 600$ The numerical value for Cosmos (ΚΟΣΜΟΣ) is 600.

$600 \times \sqrt{2} = 849$ The numerical value for Macrocosm (ΜΕΤΑΕ ΚΟΣΜΟΣ) is 849.

600 × 3 = 1040   The numerical value for Microcosm
(ΜΙΚΡΟΖ ΚΟΣΜΟΚS) is 1040.

A Father of the Church, Augustine of Hippo, said, ". . . numbers are the thoughts of God. . . . The Divine Wisdom is reflected in the numbers impressed on all things . . . the construction of the physical and moral world alike is built on eternal numbers."[5]

The concept of the Alpha and Omega is also very common in all forms of gematria, meaning the macrocosm and the microcosm, the beginning and the end. This is used in Revelation 1:8, 21:6, and 22:13. It also appears in Isaiah 44:6: "Thus says the Lord . . . I am the first and the last; besides me there is no god." God is both the unity and the multiplicity. God brings all multiplicity into unity. It's likely that the Book of Revelation is also concerned with bringing multiplicity into unity.

The relationship between multiplicity and unity was a major issue in ancient thought. The Greek Neoplatonist Proclus (412–85) spoke about the whole, parts, and harmony, the same ideas John would have been working with. "To divide and produce wholes into parts, and to preside over the distribution of forms, is Dionysiacal; but to perfect all things harmonically is Apollonical."[6] The art of achieving harmony was the ultimate goal for Proclus:

Just as [true] lovers move on beyond the beauty perceived through the senses until they reach the sole cause of all beauty and all perception, so too, the experts in sacred matters, starting with the sympathy connecting visible things both to one another and to the Invisible Powers, and having understood that all things are to be found in all things, established the Sacred Science. They marveled at seeing those things which come last in those which come first, and vice-versa; earthly things in the

*heavens in a causal and celestial manner and heavenly things
on earth in a terrestrial way.[7]*

Geometrical forms are also an important part of gematria interpretation. The Book of Revelation is obviously based on the geometric form of the circle, since Revelation refers so openly to the zodiac, which appears in a circle. In Pythagorean thought, the circle symbolized unity, and multiplicity was seen to happen within the circle of unity. So in his reference to a circle, John is probably symbolically talking about a return to unity through an achievement of harmony. We will see that this is an accurate description of the time of peace predicted in scripture.

The importance of geometrical symbols in this is summed up in this quote from Galileo:

*Philosophy is written in the great book that is ever before our
eyes—I mean the universe—but we cannot understand it if we
do not learn the language and grasp the symbols in which it is
written. This book is written in the mathematical language,
and the symbols are triangles, circles, and other geometrical figures, without whose help it is impossible to comprehend a single word of it; without which one wanders in vain through a
dark labyrinth.[8]*

The way of thinking in this worldview is different from our way of thinking about reality. Fideler calls the Greek philosophic thinking "hieroglyphic," and modern Western thought "analytic." Hieroglyphic thinking is still prevalent in much of the East and Middle East, and accounts for much misunderstanding between those areas and the West. Hieroglyphic thought always keeps the focus on unity. Separate parts of the whole can never really be understood outside the context of the whole. Real knowledge always resides in the whole. So you can't really understand any part of creation without understanding the Creator.

As a result, Fideler writes, the Greeks looked for relationships instead of for calculations. For example, if we were considering the numbers 1, 2, and 3 in hieroglyphic thought, we would look at the interrelationships among these three numbers. What are the ratios among them? How do they relate to each other? If we consider the same numbers in analytic thought, we would start with calculations. These numbers add up to 6. The analytic focus is on understanding the parts of the whole and is based on the belief that the parts can be understood as parts, without considering the whole. To understand the use of numbers by biblical writers, we have to think hieroglyphically and look for interrelationships in terms of parallels, ratios, and geometrical figures. It made sense to them that words with the same numerical value were related, in a way that is difficult for us to understand.

This system of interpretation of the gematria would not have been widely known, but was only for those who had been trained in it. The early Christian writer Origen said, "The existence of certain doctrines, which are beyond those which are exoteric and do not reach the multitude, is not a peculiarity of Christian doctrine only, but is shared by the philosophers. For they had some doctrines which were exoteric and some esoteric."[9] Clement of Alexandra agreed with him: "It is not wished that all things should be exposed indiscriminately to all and sundry, or the benefits of wisdom communicated to those who have not even in a dream been purified in soul . . . nor are the mysteries of the Word [Logos] to be expounded to the profane."[10]

In the first century mystery schools were very popular, as was the idea that one had to pass through levels before one could have certain information. That is why John says in Revelation that "those who know" understand that 666 is a human number or number of a man (depending on the translation). He obviously does know, having been trained in the gematria, and understands the significance of 666, which, as we will see, is more than and different from what most interpreters have thought.

CHAPTER 4

BIBLE SYMBOLISM

THE SYMBOLISM OF NUMBERS

As we have seen in the last chapter, numbers and form had a great deal of importance for people in antiquity. They disagreed with each other about their gods and the form of their worship, but they agreed that numbers and geometric form were important in understanding the universe. For those who were trained in the art of interpreting numbers, numbers had very specific meanings. This means that people in antiquity could talk to one another in a code language, the language of numbers. This was a code only the initiated could understand. Unless we understand this code as well, we will not be able to understand the meaning of biblical prophecy.

ONE

One was the number of God in Hebrew thought. There was one God alone (Deut. 6:4). It was also the number of unity in Greek thought, and unity was the highest good. In Christianity, there was also one people of God (Jn. 10:16; Eph. 4:4).

TWO

This was the number of duality in both Greek and Hebrew thought. Duality could be oppositional, like good and evil, right and wrong. It could also be complementary, like male and female, night and day.

THREE

The number three has more than one meaning. In the Old Testament it is sometimes the number of God's actions. God appears as three visitors (Gen. 18:2), and God announces that he will come to the people on the third day (Exod. 19:11). In Christianity, three becomes the first sacred number of completion or fullness. The Trinity is made up of the Father, the Son, and the Holy Sprit. There are three crosses at the crucifixion, and Christ rises on the third day after death. In Greek thought, three was also a number of completion, with the beginning, the middle, and the end.

FOUR

Four was considered to be the number of Creation or of the Cosmos or natural world in all of the ancient cultures. There were four elements: Fire, Earth, Air, and Water; four compass points: North, South, East, and West; four corners of the earth; the four winds (Dan. 7:2); four rivers of Eden (Gen. 2:10); and four creatures in scriptural images (Rev. 4:6). There were also four evil empires, and four Gospels for the world. The geometric form associated with the natural world was the square, which had four sides.

SIX

There is no meaning associated with the number five, but the number six is very important. As we will see, seven is a divine number, and six is one short of seven. It is a number of incompletion and imperfection. This is a number closely associated with humans, who were created on the sixth day. They also work six days a week (Luke 13:14), so this is the number of human effort. A Hebrew slave worked for six years and then was freed.

SEVEN

Seven is the most divine number of completion in the Bible. Creation was completed in seven days. God rested on the seventh day, and he decreed that humanity should also rest and worship him on the seventh day (Gen. 2:1–3). There are seven days in a week and seven-day Jewish festivals. In the Hebrew tradition, the seventh year was a sabbatical (a tradition carried on in academia), and in the sabbatical year, debts were remitted. A jubilee (fifty) was the year following seven times seven years. The Hebrew people were to praise God seven times a day (Ps. 119:164). Virtually all people in antiquity believed that there were seven visible planets, and so seven heavenly influences on the earth.

EIGHT

Eight was not used as often as other numbers in the Bible, but it had some important meanings. In two cases it was the number of a new beginning. The eighth day is the Jewish day of circumcision (Exod. 22:30), and on the eighth day, Jesus ascended into heaven to take his place at the side of the father (Jn. 20:26).

TEN

Nine is not given a meaning, but ten is a very important number. Ten is the number of completion in the human world. Just as the human has ten fingers and toes, there are ten Commandments, ten Patriarchs before the flood, ten plagues on Egypt, ten virgins

(Matt. 25:1), ten coins (Luke 15:8), and people are to tithe one-tenth of what they have to God. Ten is the basis of several number systems and appears in calculations for the Temple.

ELEVEN

Because twelve is a number of wholeness, eleven is a number of incompleteness. Only eleven apostles remain after Judas's death, and a twelfth must be chosen.

TWELVE

This is a complete number. There are twelve months in the year, twelve hours in the day, twelve tribes of Israel, and twelve apostles of Jesus. Twelve makes a whole unit, so when we see the number twelve, we know we are talking about the whole of whatever is being discussed. Twelve is also the basis of a major number system still in use today, with twelve inches to a foot, a dozen eggs in a carton. Efforts to change to a purely decimal, or ten-based, system have been resisted, since twelve is a very deeply rooted number in modern consciousness.

TWENTY-FOUR

This is a number of wholeness and restoration in Christian thought, just as twenty-four hours make a complete day. Christianity has always considered itself the continuation of Judaism, so the twelve tribes of Israel and the twelve apostles of Jesus together make twenty-four, for the restoration of the Kingdom of God.

THIRTY

There are thirty days in a month in a lunar calendar, which is the basis of astrological calculation. A circle also divides into twelve sections of thirty. A circle symbolizes unity, so unity consists of a multiple of wholeness.

FORTY

In the Bible, forty is a number meaning a lot or a long time. Israel's march through the desert lasts for forty years. Jesus is tempted for forty days. Jesus also ascends into heaven forty days after his resurrection (Acts 1–3).

FORTY-TWO

Forty-two months is three and one half years and 1,260 days. As we will see in the section on symbolic time, these are not exact calculations. Since the number three and a half is half the complete number seven, this is a number of incompletion.

144

The number 144 is the result of multiplying twelve times twelve. Twelve is a number of wholeness, and 144 is a number of perfect— or whole—wholeness. The number 144 means all of God's people. In the Old Testament, 144,000 is used to mean a large number.

1,000

Multiples of ten and of ten times ten give further meaning to the idea of worldly completion. The number 1,000 is ten times ten times ten, so it is a number of full completion. Larger numbers used in the Bible are often multiples of this number and signify the original number, plus the meaning of full completion. The number 7,000 would carry the meaning of divine completion fully carried out on earth. The number 12,000 is a number of a complete whole, and 144,000 is a perfectly complete whole.

The number 1,000 is also a signifier of a large number or length of time (Gen. 20:16; Deut. 32:30). Since the number 10,000 was the largest number used in antiquity, 1,000 is very large indeed.

1,260

This number is the number of days in three and a half years. As we will see in the section on time, time can mean days, weeks, months, or years, no matter what the text actually says.

10,000

The number 10,000 was also called a myriad, a word we still use today. It was the largest number used in antiquity.

NUMBERS IN THE BOOK OF REVELATION

Because the Book of Revelation has the most specific dating for End Time events, it is worth taking a look at how the writer, John, uses numbers.

The number one is often used to single out the actor in some event. For example, one of the elders speaks (7:13), one head of the beast receives a deathblow (13:3), and one of seven angels with bowls comes to speak (17:1). Those who join the Antichrist also have one mind (17:13), and so plagues come in one day (18:8), all is laid waste in one hour (18:10), and one mighty angel defeats Babylon (18:21).

The number two symbolizes both sides in a two-edged sword (1:16; 2:12), and the woman who gives birth to the Messiah has two wings (12:14), while one beast has two horns (13:11). It also means two woes to come (9:12) and two witnesses of God (11:3).

There are three plagues for a third of humanity (9:18) and three foul spirits (16:13). Babylon splits into three parts when she falls (16:19), and there are three gates on each wall of the New Jerusalem (21:13).

There are four living creatures in the vision (4:8; 5:6), four angels are at four corners of the earth holding back four winds (7:1), four angels are released to kill a third of humanity (9:15), and Satan will deceive the nations at the four corners of the earth (20:8).

The number of the Beast is 666.

There are seven churches and seven spirits (1:4), seven golden lamp stands (1:12), seven stars (1:20), seven seals (5:1), seven heads and eyes on the slaughtered lamb (5:6), seven angels with seven trumpets (8:6), seven thunders (10:3), 7,000 people killed in an earthquake (11:13); seven heads and diadems on the dragon (12:3), seven heads on the beast (13:1), seven angels with seven plagues (15:1), seven angels with seven bowls (16:1), seven mountains in Babylon (17:9), and seven kings (17:10).

Some beasts also have ten horns and ten diadems (13:1), and there are ten kings (17:16).

There are twelve stars on the woman's head (12:1), twelve gates in the walls of the new Jerusalem and twelve tribes of Israel (21:12), twelve foundation stones for the new city with the names of the twelve apostles (21:14), and each of the twelve gates has a pearl (21:21).

Around the throne of God there are twenty-four thrones upon which are seated twenty-four elders (4:4). The elders fall down and worship God (5:8; 11:16; 19:4).

The nations will trample the courtyard of the temple for forty-two months (11:2), and the beast will speak haughty words and exercise authority for forty-two months (13:5).

The wall of the new city is 144 cubits (21:17), 144,000 are sealed by an angel (7:4), and 144,000 stand with Jesus on Mt. Zion

(14:1). A total of 12,000 are sealed from each of the twelve tribes of Israel (7:6–8).

There is one fractional number that is particularly important, and that is one-third. This is used to describe the damage that is done to the earth. One-third of the following is destroyed: earth and trees burned up (8:7), sea becomes blood, living creatures in sea die, ships destroyed (8:9), waters become wormwood (8:11), sun, moon, and stars darkened (8:12), humanity killed (9:15, 9:18), and stars fall (12:4).

John's very consistent symbolic use of numbers makes it clear that he isn't using numbers literally. He doesn't mean that one-third of humanity will necessarily die. He means that a large and significant portion of humanity will be killed and a large and significant portion of the environment—the air, water, trees—will be damaged before the Apocalypse is over.

THE SYMBOLISM OF TIME IN THE BIBLE

Prophecy depends a great deal on the understanding of time, and that makes biblical prophecy difficult to understand. Time in the Bible, like numbers, was often symbolic. In the New Testament, references to time were sometimes a reference back to the Old Testament rather than a literal statement of time. These references had more to do with showing a connection to ancient tradition than with predicting the future.

In the Old Testament, time was not always meant literally either. For example, Jeremiah predicted that Babylon would destroy Jerusalem and then be punished in seventy years (25:11). Daniel (9:24–27) clarified that this really meant seventy *weeks* of years, or 490 years. This didn't seem so strange in Hebrew culture, because numbers of years, like other numbers, had symbolic meaning. A week of years, or forty-nine years, made up a jubilee, and a jubilee year was celebrated at the fiftieth year. A period of 490 years was ten jubilees, a significant number of divine completion. It was common to think in terms of ten periods of time.

So when we see numbers of time in the Bible, they might be symbolic, particularly the numbers seven, three and a half (half of seven), and ten. Even if the numbers are intended to be literal periods of time, we don't know what unit of time they are. A number could refer to days, weeks, months, years, weeks of years, or decades, even if it purports to be some other unit of time. This will give us some challenges in calculating the events of the twenty-first century.

Numbers are essential to understanding predictions of the future, but we cannot be too literal in our understanding of what numbers mean. Many of the most widespread beliefs about the End Time in popular culture or popular literature are based on literal interpretation of numbers in biblical texts; numbers that clearly had symbolic meaning for both the writers and people reading those texts. Whenever we see numbers, we need to stop and ask ourselves if the number is meant literally, symbolically, or to link the text to another text. Only when we do that can we have a hope of understanding what the biblical writers meant to tell us.

CHAPTER 5

BABYLON THE BEAST

FOUR EVIL EMPIRES

As we saw in chapter 1, there are several events connected to the End Time by biblical prophecy. The first we will look at is the evil nation or beast-nation that will threaten humanity. There is much talk of beasts in biblical prophecy, and to understand how this image is used, it is important to know the story of Nebuchadnezzar (also spelled Nebuchadrezzar from the Babylonian Nabu-Kudurri-usar, "the god Nabu has protected the succession") and the Jewish captivity in Babylon.

In the seventh century B.C.E., Judah was a kingdom of what is now southern Israel, and this kingdom was under the control of Egypt. In 627, a new dynasty was founded in the great city of Babylon by Nebuchadnezzar's father, Nabopolassar. Babylon had been an ally of Egypt, but when Nebuchadnezzar came to power in 605, he turned against Egypt and defeated it. Babylon then took control of Egypt's former possessions, including the kingdom of Judah. Four years later, the king of Judah, Jehoiakim, stopped paying tribute to Babylon. Some say it was because he mistakenly thought Egypt was regaining its power in the region. In retaliation, Nebuchadnezzar besieged Jerusalem in 597. The king of Judah died and his son by the same name surrendered. Nebuchadnezzar took the new king and others captive to Babylon along with the sacred vessels from the Temple. He installed a new king, Zedekiah, who rebelled a few years later. Nebuchadnezzar was furious at the second rebellion, and he sacked Jerusalem, destroyed the temple, slaughtered many, destroyed the land, and took more captives to Babylon.

One of the Hebrew people in captivity in Babylon, according to the Old Testament, was a man named Daniel, who was from a family of the Judean nobility and was born about the time of King Josiah's religious renewal, which dates to about 622 B.C.E. He was included in the captives taken to Babylon by king Nebuchadnezzar around 600, taken with three friends, Shadrach, Meshack, and Abednego. Daniel appears to have studied with the Chaldeans and became recognized as a wise man at the Babylonian court of Nebuchadnezzar, eventually rising to the post of chief wise man. His last recorded vision was in 586, when he would have been in his mid-eighties.

Daniel encouraged the Hebrew people to renew their trust in God. His visions revealed the intention of God to send the Son of Man (7:13) to establish a millennial reign. Daniel is credited with predicting the Greek defeat of Persia (8:20–21), the persecution of Judah by Antiochus Epiphanes, which occurred from 168 to 165 B.C.E. (8:9–14, 23–26), and the first coming of Jesus (9:25).

The Book of Daniel is the last and the shortest of the four major books of prophets in the Old Testament, containing fifty-eight separate prophecies. Still, the prophecies of Daniel are sweeping, and Daniel is one of the Bible's leading books of apocalyptic literature, along with Zechariah and the Book of Revelation.

Some modern scholars dispute the date of the sixth-century B.C.E. for this book. The predictions of Daniel are remarkably accurate up to about 164 B.C.E., and are much less accurate after that, so scholars date the text to around 164. As further evidence of this dating, they point out that a list of Jewish heroes made by Ben Sira in about 180 B.C.E. does not include Daniel, but the list found in 1 Maccabees 2:59–60, dated about 100 B.C.E., includes both Daniel and his three companions.

Despite scholarly criticism and commentary, the Book of Daniel provides the basis for much of current popular biblical prophecy. Daniel rose to fame in Babylon by interpreting a dream of Nebuchadnezzar's. Nebuchadnezzar had a dream that frightened him, and he demanded that the wise men of Babylon tell him the meaning of the dream without hearing what the dream was. When they told him that wasn't possible, he ordered them executed. To save the wise men from execution, Daniel asked God for the interpretation of the dream, which God gave to him. The dream symbolized four kingdoms, starting with Nebuchadnezzar's own. At the end of the fourth kingdom, a new kingdom of God would be set up that would never end (Dan. 2:36–45).

Later, Daniel had his own dream in which he saw four beasts come out of the sea. The fourth beast was the strongest, just as the fourth beast in Nebuchadnezzar's dream had been the strongest. It had ten horns, with human eyes in the horns, and a mouth speaking arrogantly:

> *After this I saw in the night visions, and behold a fourth beast, dreadful and terrible, and strong exceedingly; and it had great iron teeth: it devoured and brake in pieces, and stamped the residue with the feet of it: and it was diverse from all the beasts that were before it; and it had ten horns. I considered the horns, and, behold, there came up among them another little horn, before whom there were three of the first horns plucked up by*

the roots: and, behold, in this horn were eyes like the eyes of man, and a mouth speaking great things (Dan. 7:7–8).

The vision continued with the Ancient of Days (God) ascending a throne, with thousands upon thousands in attendance. He destroyed all four of the beasts and then the Messiah came and was given dominion over all nations that would never end:

I saw in the night visions, and, behold, one like the Son of man came with the clouds of heaven, and came to the Ancient of days, and they brought him near before him. And there was given him dominion, and glory, and a kingdom, that all people, nations, and languages, should serve him: his dominion is an everlasting dominion, which shall not pass away, and his kingdom that which shall not be destroyed (Dan. 7:13–14).

Daniel was confused about the meaning of this dream, and one of the attendants of the Ancient of Days explained the meaning of the fourth beast to him:

Thus he said, The fourth beast shall be the fourth kingdom upon earth, which shall be diverse from all kingdoms, and shall devour the whole earth, and shall tread it down, and break it in pieces.

And the ten horns out of this kingdom are ten kings that shall arise: and another shall rise after them; and he shall be diverse from the first, and he shall subdue three kings.

And he shall speak great words against the most High, and shall wear out the saints of the most High, and think to change times and laws: and they shall be given into his hand until a time and times and the dividing of time.

> *But the judgment shall sit, and they shall take away his do-*
> *minion, to consume and to destroy it unto the end.*
>
> *And the kingdom and dominion, and the greatness of the*
> *kingdom under the whole heaven, shall be given to the people*
> *of the saints of the most High, whose kingdom is an everlast-*
> *ing kingdom, and all dominions shall serve and obey him*
> *(Dan. 7:23–27).*

Most modern scholars identify the four kingdoms in Daniel with the four empires: Babylonian, Persian, Greek, and Roman. Rome was the strongest and most destructive and would conquer the whole world as they knew it. The horns are usually thought to mean ten Roman emperors. It is fairly clear that the early Christians of the first century also interpreted Daniel in this way.

As we've already noted, the symbolism and mythology used in Hebrew and Christian writings often resembled or was borrowed from the mythology of people around them. The beast rising out of the sea in Daniel's dream resembles the story from Canaanite mythology in which the earth was troubled by a sea monster named Rehab. In the process of creation, God dried the sea and smote Rehab.[1] In the Old Testament there is a similar figure, an evil serpent named Leviathan. In Isaiah there is promise that God will kill Leviathan along with the dragon in the sea (Isa. 27:1). Of course, the images of the serpent and the dragon are associated with Satan throughout Jewish and Christian thought. The themes of these stories, therefore, are all the same. God promises to eventually destroy evil and to turn the government of the earth over to the representative of good, the Messiah.

By the time of the advent of Christianity, this story was widely known, and Babylon and the succeeding empires had been associated with the image of the beast for hundreds of years. Rome, as the fourth empire in the succession, was linked to Babylon by this association and was believed to be the last empire that would exist before the Messianic age. After Rome sacked Jerusalem in 70 C.E.—as Babylon had done over six and a half centuries before—it was sometimes called Babylon by both Jews and Christians.[2]

Babylon was also associated with the image of the whore or harlot. In Jeremiah 23, God calls Samaria and Jerusalem—the kingdoms of Israel and Judah—whores or harlots because they have worshiped the gods of Egypt, Assyria, and Babylon. Though sexual imagery is used, the offense is clearly the offense of consorting with pagan gods. For this the Hebrew kingdoms are condemned to destruction by Assyria and Babylon.

Babylon, which worshiped pagan gods, was called a harlot for the same reason. Babylon was also associated with the goddess/demoness Tiamat (sometimes Tiamut), which strengthened the connection with a pagan female figure, or harlot. Tiamat was a figure in the Babylonian creation epic called *Enuma Elish*. In the beginning of creation in this story, there was only water. Tiamat was salt water and the male god Apsu was fresh water. They mated and produced a brood of gods and goddesses and then a brood of monsters. Tiamat was the original mother of all. The offspring fought and created war. Eventually, Tiamat's great-great-grandson, Marduk, fought and killed Tiamat. He then cut her dead body in half and used the upper half to create the heavens and the lower half to create the earth. So the primordial ocean (Tiamat) from which all the Babylonian gods were born was also the source of the cosmos and physical world. Tiamat had a host of dragons and was portrayed in dragon form. She is the dragon that rises out of the primordial ocean of herself. To the very patriarchal Hebrews, this essential feminine role in creation must have looked demonic indeed. This myth was the basis of the way the Hebrews saw the Babylonians and very influential in the Hebrews' mythical portrayal of evil.

There was another similarity between Babylon and Rome, and that is that both of them were located on rivers. Babylon is referred to in Jeremiah 50:38 and 51:13 as a city on many waters. Rome, located on the Tiber River, was also located on many waters.

NERO AND THE FIRE IN ROME

The Roman emperor Nero was a great-grandson of Caesar Augustus. When he was a child, he and his mother, Agrippina, were exiled to the tiny Pontian Islands by his uncle, Gaius Caligula. A few years later, Agrippina's uncle Claudius became emperor, and Agrippina convinced Claudius to marry her and make Nero heir to the empire. Claudius was then murdered—legend says Agrippina gave him poisoned mushrooms. Nero became the emperor in 54 C.E., at the age of sixteen. Several years later, he had his mother moved to another residence, where she was killed. The rumor circulated that Nero had killed his own mother.

Nero had a grand plan to tear down about a third of Rome and to build a series of palaces to be known as the Neropolis. Unfortunately for Nero, the Senate didn't agree to his plan. On the night of July 19, 64 C.E., a major fire broke out in Rome, and rumor said that Nero had the fire started to clear space for his projects.

Slums, which covered much of the city, were fire hazards, and the fire raged for six days before it could be gotten under control, only to reignite and burn for two more days. When it was over, two-thirds of Rome was destroyed, including the eight-hundred-year-old Temple of Jupiter Stator and the hearth of the Vestal Virgins.

Nero was away in the cooler coastal town of Antium at the time of the fire, but the historian Tacitus claims Nero merrily played the fiddle while Rome burned. Tacitus was only a boy at the time of the fire, and he was reporting legends rather than first-hand observation. His reports show that the tendency to blame Nero for the fire was widespread. Tacitus's report was that Nero's thugs prevented citizens from fighting the fire and threatened them.

Nero blamed the fire on what was then a small, obscure sect in Rome called Christians. There is evidence that in 64 many Roman Christians believed in prophecies that Rome would be destroyed by fire. If this evidence is accurate, it may explain why Nero chose this group as a scapegoat to blame for the fire. He may have hoped to deflect suspicion from himself. The Christians were subjected to torture and horrible deaths so that Nero could make an example of them.

After the fire Nero began to collect vast sums of money from individuals and vassal states, using the fire as an excuse. The Domus Aurea, a series of villas and pavilions on a landscaped park and man-made lake, was built in the wake of the fire.

In the Book of Revelation, John sees a beast rising out of the water, which has the characteristics of all four beasts in Daniel's dream. In addition, it has not only ten horns but seven heads. The horns are also crowned, strengthening the connection to kingdoms or rulers of some kind. The beast is speaking arrogantly (Rev. 12:18–13:8). A little later, a great whore is seated on the beast, and on her forehead is written "Babylon the great, mother of Whores and of earth's abominations." She also sits on many waters (Rev. 17:1–6). An angel explains this vision to John. The seven heads are seven mountains and seven kings, five of whom had fallen, one was living, and one was to come. The water was multitudes, and the ten horns were the kingdoms that would destroy the whore and the beast (Rev. 17:9–18).

Here the harlot is not only Babylon but also Rome, which was famous for its seven hills and location on the water. The seven kings probably refer to seven Roman emperors, and John expects only one more after the one then living, probably Domitian.

The expectation of many early Christians was that the Messiah would come at the end of the Roman Empire, just as the Messiah came after God destroyed the fourth beast in Daniel's dream. Many of them expected that to happen in their own lifetimes. Paul mentions this many times in his writings. In the apocryphal Epistle of Barnabas, which was probably written between 70 and 75, about twenty years before the Book of Revelation was written, the author quotes Daniel's description of the beast and expects the events described there to happen in his own time.[3]

Of course, we know that the Roman Empire did fall eventually, though not for several centuries. Still, when the Roman Empire fell, the Messiah did not come back physically to take control and rule the world. What does this mean for the accuracy or usefulness of prophecy? Many interpreters of biblical prophecy see the prophecies as repeating. They expect a new beast to arise, or perhaps a new series of four beasts, before the Messiah returns. The nation or empire beast that is related to Babylon and Rome is also associated with the Antichrist, whom we will discuss in the next chapter.

AN EMPIRE BEAST IN OUR TIME

With the benefit of two thousand years of hindsight, we can see that there have been many corrupt nations and empires and attempts to take over the world since the time of the Roman Empire. In recent history, the example that stands out is the alliance of Germany, Italy, and Japan, the Axis powers that were defeated in World War II. As we will see, there is reason to believe that Adolph Hitler, the most prominent figure in the Axis powers, was an Antichrist.

The capital of Nazi Germany was Berlin, a city located on the Elbe, as well as other smaller waterways. Berlin was the location of the German Command during the war, where directions were given in the effort to take over the world. Orders were also given from there for mass executions of millions of people.

We have seen that the prophecy of bestial empires and leaders has repeated many times, so does this mean that another nation beast will arise before the End Time? If so, how can we recognize it? We can expect that a beast-nation will be a whore in that it will worship a false god. In modern terms, that may mean the worship of Mammon or money. A nation that believes material wealth is more important than people, the environment, ethics, moral principles, or spiritual values would be a good candidate for a beast. We can also expect that a future nation beast will have the other characteristics of the Babylonian, Persian, Greek, and Roman empires, as well as those of the Axis alliance. For example, this nation or empire will believe in its own superiority and be contemptuous of others. It will have no respect for individual freedom, human life, or religious difference. It will believe that its own superiority entitles it to conquer and control the world, and will be willing to use any method to gain that end, however brutal. In modern terms, this nation would probably be willing to use horrible weapons, including atomic bombs.

In the sixteenth century the prophet Nostradamus foretold an Antichrist figure he called "Hister," or Hitler. He said that only divine intervention could stop Hitler, and maybe it did. The "impossible" D day invasion of the Normandy coast succeeded and changed the course of the war. Some kind of divine intervention might also be needed to stop a beast-nation armed with nuclear weapons and willing to use them to destroy the world. And that intervention is what the Bible promises.

CHAPTER 6

THE SECOND BEAST: THE ANTICHRIST

THE NUMBER OF THE BEAST

We saw in the last chapter that Old Testament prophecy and the Book of Revelation identified nations or empires with beasts. The Book of Revelation also identifies a second Beast, a beast in the form of a human. We know this from Revelation 13:18, where John describes the mark of the Beast as the number 666, and identifies it as human. Bible translators differ on what this phrase of Revelation actually says. The King James Bible translation says, "Here is wisdom. Let him that hath understanding count the number of the beast: for it is the number of a man; and his number is Six hundred threescore and six," while the New Revised Standard Version says, "This calls for wisdom: let anyone with understanding calculate the number of the beast, for it is the number of a person. Its number is six hundred sixty-six." This means that the Beast could be a person, a human characteristic, or both. We shall see that for John it was both.

This Beast has been equated with the prophecies for an Antichrist. The word Antichrist actually appears only once in the Bible, in 1 John 2:18. "Little children, it is the last time: and as ye have heard that antichrist shall come, even now are there many antichrists; whereby we know that it is the last time." It is clear in that text that John is not only expecting several antichrist figures, not just one, but he thinks they have already arrived. This is not the second Beast John refers to in Revelation, because that figure is expected in the future. Still, most people call the second beast in the Book of Revelation the Antichrist, so that's what we will call him.

This Beast or Antichrist comes in each cycle of the Apocalypse, as we will see. If the prototype first Beast was Babylon, the prototype for the first Antichrist should be Nebuchadnezzar. If that is so, we should find that the number of his name is 666. Sure enough, Nebuchadnezzar in Greek (ΝΗΒΗΚΗΔΝΗΣΣΗΡ) has a numerical value of 666.[1]

If John saw Rome as the nation beast of his time, as he clearly did, then the Antichrist of his time was associated with Rome. In the seven letters to the seven churches in Revelation John spoke of persecution of the churches, so the Beast was most likely a Roman emperor who persecuted Christians. The Roman emperor of John's time most associated with persecution of Christians was Nero. According to the historian Tacitus, Nero blamed the Christians for the fire that destroyed Rome in 64, and he slaughtered many of them in revenge. The historian Eusebius also writes that Nero beheaded Paul and crucified Peter upside down.[2] Given these actions against the Christians of Rome and against the most well known early Christian leaders, no one would have looked more like a Beast or Antichrist to the early Christians than Nero.

John would not have missed the fact that Nero's name, like Nebuchadnezzar's, was associated with 666. In Greek, Nero Caesar (ΝΕΡΩΝ ΚΑΕΣΑΡ) is the numerical equivalent of 1332, which is 666 times 2. Prophecy writer Lynn Louise Schuldt writes that J. C. Rolfe translates Nero's natural name in Latin as "Lucios Domitium

Aheno-barborum," which is the equivalent of 666.[3] We know these kinds of calculations were common at the time, since Suetonius tells us of a first-century graffiti in Rome that said:

Count the numerical value
Of the letters in Nero's name,
And in "murdered his own mother."
You will find their sum is the same.[4]

This tells us that everyone who could read Latin would have known that Nero's name in Latin, like Nebuchadnezzar's in Greek, was equivalent to 666. Nero's name in Hebrew, Nron Qsar, was also equivalent to 666,[5] effectively identifying him as a Beast or Antichrist.

Nero was almost certainly already dead when John wrote Revelation, but Tactitus and Suetonius tell us that there was a commonly held belief after his death in 68 that he would come back to life and rule again.[6] Many commentators have connected that legend to the language of Revelation 13:3: "And I saw one of his heads as it were wounded to death; and his deadly wound was healed: and all the world wondered after the beast." It is possible that John was expecting Nero to return and to provoke the battle of Armageddon, but it is also possible that his vision included more Antichrists/Beasts in the future.

Throughout history there have been many nominees for the position of Antichrist. The early Christian writer Hippolytus (170–236) chose Antiochus Epiphanes, the emperor Augustus, and one more to come in the future. The sixteenth-century prophet Nostradamus identified three Antichrists: Napoleon, Hitler, and a third Antichrist he called Mabus, whom we have not yet identified.

Many commentators have named Adolf Hitler as an Antichrist figure, with good reason. We will see that Hitler not only has many of the qualifications of a Beast, but the events of World War II go a long way toward fulfilling many apocalyptic prophecies. Hitler's name does not add up to 666, but the numerical value of the name Adolf Hitler and the name of his birthplace Austria together in Hebrew (הירסטוא רלטיה פלודא) equals 666. Also, Adolf Hitler in Hebrew (רלטיה פלודא) has the numerical value of 375, which adds up to 6, in a calculation called theosophical gematria.[7] This is not as exact a match as Nero, but it is still the most convincing connection to the number 666 for any Antichrist figure since Nero's time.

If Nebuchadnezzar, Nero, Hitler, and quite possibly others were all Beasts or Antichrist figures, this tells us that the prophecies for an Antichrist figure were not prophecies of a one-time event but prophecies of a reoccurring cycle. This leads us to look for clues to how we can get out of this cycle and move toward the return of the Messiah. We will look at that in more detail in later chapters. For now, we can ask what information we have to identify Antichrists in our own time or the future.

THE NATURE OF THE SECOND BEAST

Unfortunately, there has been a tendency in past decades to use the image of the Beast and the number 666 to attack religious rivals. Some Protestants identified the Pope as an Antichrist, while a former Pope claimed that the name "Mohamet" has a numerical value of 666. For this reason, it is important to look beyond the number 666 to understand the nature of the Beast, so we can identify real Antichrist figures. What do Nebuchadnezzar, Nero, and Hitler have in common? They are literally satanic figures, in that they try to replace God and they do this in a particularly vicious way.

Paul agrees with this description of the anti-messiah figure that will come before the Messiah. In his second letter to the Thessalonians, Paul calls this person the man of lawlessness. In 2 Thessalonians 2: 4 he writes, "Who opposeth and exalteth himself above all that is called God, or that is worshipped; so that he as God sitteth in the temple of God, shewing himself that he is God."

John, too, in the story of the woman and the Dragon in Rev. 12, makes it clear that the Antichrist is trying to usurp the place of the Messiah:

And there appeared a great wonder in heaven; a woman clothed with the sun, and the moon under her feet, and upon her head a crown of twelve stars: And she being with child cried, travailing in birth, and pained to be delivered. And there appeared another wonder in heaven; and behold a great red dragon, having seven heads and ten horns, and seven crowns upon his heads. And his tail drew the third part of the stars of heaven, and did cast them to the earth: and the dragon stood before the woman which was ready to be delivered, for to devour her child as soon as it was born. And she brought forth a man-child, who was to rule all nations with a rod of iron: and her child was caught up unto God, and to his throne. And the woman fled into the wilderness, where she hath a place prepared of God, that they should feed her there a thousand two hundred and threescore days.

And there was war in heaven: Michael and his angels fought against the dragon; and the dragon fought and his angels, And prevailed not; neither was their place found any more in heaven. And the great dragon was cast out, that old serpent, called the Devil, and Satan, which deceiveth the whole world: he was cast out into the earth, and his angels were cast out with him.

And I heard a loud voice saying in heaven, Now is come salvation, and strength, and the kingdom of our God, and the power of his Christ: for the accuser of our brethren is cast down, which accused them before our God day and night.

And they overcame him by the blood of the Lamb, and by the word of their testimony; and they loved not their lives unto the death.

Therefore rejoice, ye heavens, and ye that dwell in them. Woe to the inhabiters of the earth and of the sea! for the devil is come down unto you, having great wrath, because he knoweth that he hath but a short time.

And when the dragon saw that he was cast unto the earth, he persecuted the woman which brought forth the man-child.

And to the woman were given two wings of a great eagle, that she might fly into the wilderness, into her place, where she is nourished for a time, and times, and half a time, from the face of the serpent.

And the serpent cast out of his mouth water as a flood after the woman, that he might cause her to be carried away of the flood.

And the earth helped the woman, and the earth opened her mouth, and swallowed up the flood which the dragon cast out of his mouth.

And the dragon was wroth with the woman, and went to make war with the remnant of her seed, which keep the commandments of God, and have the testimony of Jesus Christ.

The Dragon tries to devour the one who is to rule the nations, the Messiah. By devouring the baby, he would usurp his place. This story was an old one and familiar to the people of John's time. In the Greek version of the story, Leto became pregnant by Zeus, but the beast Python pursued her and tried to kill her. She was protected by the North Wind and Poseidon, the god of the Sea. She gave birth to Apollo, who grew up to defeat Python, thus becoming a savior figure.

In the Egyptian version, Isis gave birth to Horus but was pursued by Seth-Typhon, who wanted to kill the child. Ra and Thoth came to the aid of Isis, and Horus survived. He grew up to defeat Seth-Typhon.[8] In the Christian telling of the story in the Book of Revelation, Satan wants to devour Jesus and take his rightful place, but Jesus is protected. He will return and defeat Satan. The message—the same in all these stories—is that the intention of Satan and of the Beast/Antichrist is to replace God, but God will always defeat the Beast.

The Jewish legend of Satan's fall says that Satan wished to compete with God and to be a God in his own right. For this, he was cast out of Paradise. The angel sent to battle Satan and who defeated him and cast him out was Michael. Michael means "Who is Equal to God?"[9] A statue in the Latin Quarter of Paris has Michael trading on the fallen form of Satan with the caption "Who Dares to Be God?"

Mortal people, too, tried to compete with God or challenge God. We see this in the story of the Tower of Babel (Gen. 11:4–9). Babel, not surprisingly, was located in the Chaldean empire or Babylon. The story says that the people there tried to build a tower that would reach to Heaven. For this, God punished them by making them speak many languages so they couldn't communicate.

Isaiah saw this trait in Nebuchadnezzar and directly accused him of trying to usurp God's place: "For thou hast said in thine heart, I will ascend into heaven, I will exalt my throne above the stars of God: I will sit also upon the mount of the congregation, in the sides of the north: I will ascend above the heights of the clouds; I will be like the most High" (Isa. 14:13–14). Throughout the Old Testament, the essential quality of the anti-God figure is an ambition to replace God. It is no surprise to find that the ambition of the anti-Messiah figure is to replace the Messiah and to replace God. In terms of monotheistic thought, this is the creature in competition with the Creator. In terms of Eastern thought, this is the ego or false self in competition with the Whole or Emptiness. Virtually every religious tradition identifies this as the greatest human evil or weakness.

We can see that our three Beasts all had this quality. Isaiah accused Nebuchadnezzar of trying to usurp God's place, and Daniel tells the story of how Nebuchadnezzar set up a golden image and demanded that people worship it or die (Dan. 3). When three Hebrew men refused, he had them cast into a fiery furnace, from which God rescued them. Nebuchadnezzar repented then, in awe, but not for long. He kept falling back into his own greed for power until God told him that his kingdom had been given to the Medes and Persians (Dan. 5:28).

The apocryphal Hebrew text, Judith, agrees with Isaiah that Nebuchadnezzar wanted to be God. The text says, "It was granted to him [Holophernes] to destroy all the gods of the area so that all the nations should worship Nebuchadnezzar alone—that every dialect and tribe should call upon him as God."[10]

All of the Roman emperors of the first century would also qualify as usurpers of God's power. The emperor was deified and people were required to worship him. According to inscriptions and papyri,

Augustus (30 B.C.E.–14 C.E.) was called "God" and "Son of God." Tiberius (14–37 C.E.) was called "son of God" and "Son of Zeus the Liberator." Nero (54–68) was called "Son of the greatest of gods" and "Lord of the whole world."[11] Even among the emperors of his time, Nero was the most self-aggrandizing.

Was Hitler, too, an Antichrist figure in this way? His hatred of Jews and Judaism is well known, but his attacks on Christianity are less well known. There is extensive evidence showing that he considered himself a Messiah who would replace Jesus and that he expected the religion of his Reich to replace Christianity.

Hermann Rauschning, president of the Nazi Senate in Danzig, reported that Hitler spoke of preaching a new Gospel to humanity.[12] In July of 1934, the Church of the Reich was created under the motto "One People, One Reich, One Faith." The following year, Hans Kerrl declared that "the Party believes in the principle of Positive Christianity and Positive Christianity is National Socialism. . . . The Fuhrer is herald of a new revelation." Articles were drawn up for the National Church, including the following: Article 13: "The National Church demands that the publication and distribution of the Bible in Germany shall cease immediately." Article 19: "There must be nothing on the altars apart from *Mein Kampf*—the most sacred of all books to every German and therefore also to God—and on the left of the altar, a sword." Article 30: "On the day this comes into effect, the Christian cross must be removed from all churches, cathedrals and chapels and replaced by the only invincible symbol, the swastika."[13]

Rauschning also claimed that Himmler told him he was founding an Order of Man-God, and, in fact, an order was formed under Himmler that had twelve Warrior priests. They believed that Nazi heroes would be resurrected to eternal life. Hitler, himself, said, "The old beliefs will be brought back to honor again, the whole secret knowledge of nature, of the divine, the demonic. We will wash off the Christian veneer, and bring out a religion peculiar to our race."[14]

This idea was echoed in a Nazi school song:

Adolf Hitler is our savior, our hero,
The noblest being in the whole world,
For Hitler we live,
For Hitler we die,
Our Hitler is our Savior
Who rules a wonderful new world.[15]

All three of these figures, then, claimed God or Messiah status, wanted to rule the world as they knew it, and wanted to be worshiped. Were they also particularly vicious?

Part of the uniqueness of the Hebrew people throughout ancient history was their tendency to resist domination by other empires. In the long history of their resistance, no ruler treated them more brutally than Nebuchadnezzar. When he decided to punish them, his intent was more to annihilate them than to subdue them. The Babylonian army not only killed and scattered the people, but it destroyed the crops and trees, and damaged the land as much as possible.

Nero, too, was known for his vicious nature. Tacitus claims that Nero used the excuse of the fire in Rome to kill Christians in various sadistic ways. He had them covered with animal skins and torn apart by dogs, nailed to crosses, and burned alive. He is said to have used burning people as torches to light a party in his garden, which he attended dressed as a charioteer.[16]

No one acquainted with the story of the Holocaust in German-occupied territory during World War II could have any doubts about the viciousness of Adolf Hitler. An estimated six million

Jews were killed under his direction, as well as several million others, including gypsies, Communists, and mental patients. The story of this slaughter is, perhaps, more vicious than any other in history, since it was carried out in a systematic way over a period of time. Prisoners were starved and forced to work until they no longer could. Special chambers were built for mass executions of those no longer useful; then the bodies were dumped into mass graves, after gold had been removed from the teeth. A few Nazis carried brutality almost beyond imagination by killing children in front of their parents and making articles, like lamp shades, out of the skin of murdered children. Few people doubt that Hitler and thousands who worked with him were essentially Beasts.

If an Antichrist is arising again in our time, then we need to watch for these characteristics: a grossly inflated idea about his power and worth, a desire to control the world, and a belief in his right to do anything, however cruel or brutal, to reach his ends. Spotting an Antichrist, however, isn't quite that simple, because, as we shall see, an Antichrist may hide those characteristics if they are unpopular. This means that we have to learn to look past public relation images, sound bites, and propaganda to see who people really are.

THE MARK OF THE BEAST

John writes in Revelation 13:11–18 that the followers of the Beast will be marked on the right hand or the forehead, and that no one can buy or sell who does not have that mark. The mark is the name or number of the Beast, and the number of the Beast is 666.

The mark of the Beast is the reverse of the mark of God described in Ezekiel, when God directed a man dressed in linen to mark the forehead of those in Jerusalem who abhorred the abominations in the city (Ezek. 9:4). God marks the 144,000 in a similar way in Revelation 7:1–8. People were anointed in the Hebrew tradition by placing oil on their forehead.

There are many theories about what John thought the mark of the Beast was in his day. The Greek word used for mark is *charagma*, which was the technical term for the Roman imperial stamp that appeared on various documents. The *charagma* was a seal stamped with the name and date of the emperor and attached to commercial documents. Apparently, it also stood for the emperor's head stamped on coins. One aspect of the mark for John was most likely Roman coins, which had the image and name of the emperor, the Beast, on them, and which were needed to buy and sell. Other early Christians also connected the mark of the Beast to coinage or the metaphor of coinage. The early Christian martyr Ignatius, who died in Rome in about 108 C.E., probably about fifteen years after Revelation was written, said this:

> *Seeing then that there is an end to all, that the choice is between two things, death and life, and that each is to go to his own place; for, just as there are two coinages, the one of God, and the other of the world, and each has its own stamp impressed on it, so the unbelievers bear the stamp of the world, and the believers the stamp of God the Father in love through Jesus Christ, and unless we willingly choose to die through him in his passion, his life is not in us.*[17]

The *charagma* was also a type of brand. In Roman times, disobedient slaves were often branded with marks of ownership, much like cattle are today. Religious tattooing was also widespread. Soldiers had a custom of branding themselves with the name of a favorite general. Devotees of a god labeled themselves with tattoos to designate their loyal devotion.

If the references to marking on the forehead in Revelation is symbolic, as it is in Ezekiel, or is referring to the customs of the first century, then we don't have to look for a literal fulfillment in the twenty-first century. If the mark is not a literal visible mark, the most important clue to what it might be in our time is the comment that no one can buy or sell without it.

This ties the Beast and the mark of the Beast to the issue of money and greed. One of the most important points all of the Old Testament prophets made was that the people were to be responsible about money and were not to engage in usury. Many commentators have suggested that the most likely mark of the Beast in our electronic age will be an electronic number. This is very possible, since many of our electronic transactions involve providers of "credit," who often charge usurious rates of interest. The connection between that and the nature of the Beast may be very real.

In the case of Nazi Germany, the mark was the swastika, a symbol stolen from Eastern religious traditions such as Buddhism and Jainism and reversed, so it could be used for evil instead of good. It is interesting that the swastika was often worn on an armband, though on the left arm. Given Hitler's interest in esoteric subjects, we can be sure he knew all about the mark of the Beast and may have intentionally mimicked it. Concentration camp inmates were tattooed with numbers on their wrists.

THE FUTURE BEAST

If we experience a Beast or Antichrist in our time, will we be able to recognize him? Nostradamus told us that Mabus will be connected to the Middle East.[18] The twentieth-century prophet Jeane Dixon claimed that the Antichrist was alive and operating in the Middle East in the 1990s. She also warned that he will be extremely popular, because he will pretend to have a great love for humanity while really harboring a satanic urge for power.[19]

In order to recognize the Antichrist for what he is before he wreacks havoc again, humanity will have to learn enough lessons about lust for power and greed so that they are able to spot the Antichrist even when he is disguised. This learning process may be an important part of a spiritual renewal that is happening now or will happen in the near future.

CHAPTER 7

JESUS AND THE BEAST

THE BEAST AND THE SUN

In the Book of Revelation, John identifies the number 666 as the number of the Beast. This number in ancient Greek culture was related to the sun. Since the Book of Revelation claims to have been written on Patmos, an island opposite Greece and heavily influenced by Greek culture, it is important to explore this more fully to understand what John was trying to communicate.

The number 666 is the sum of 1 to 36, the numbers that make up the magical square of the sun. These squares of the planets were considered magical because each line of numbers in the square added up to the same total. For the square of the sun, each line totaled 111. There were seven magical squares associated with the seven visible planets: Saturn, Jupiter, Mars, Sun, Venus, Mercury, and the Moon. The squares contained the following numbers, arranged in such a way that the sum of any vertical, horizontal, or diagonal line was the same:

Saturn: 1–9, line = 15
Jupiter: 1–16, line = 34

Mars: 1–25, line = 65

Sun: 1–36; line = 111

Venus: 1–48, line = 175

Mars: 1–64, line = 260

Moon: 1–80; line = 369.

The ancient practice of gematria, in which the names of deities had significant numerical values, also connected the number 666 to the sun. The name of the spirit of the Sun in Hebrew was So-rath (תרוס), which had a numerical value of 666. The intelligence of the Sun was Nakiel (לאיכנ), with a numerical value of 111. The ancient Greek solar deity Teitan (**TEITAN**) also had the numerical value of 666. So both the numbers 666 and 111 had been associated with the sun for a long time and across cultures.

In ancient pagan cultures, the sun, moon, and five other visible planets were worshipped as actual gods. Aristotle and Plato, for example, thought the heavenly bodies were divine. Aristotle believed the cosmos was made up of concentric spheres consisting of four elements: earth, air, fire, and water. Changes in heavenly bodies changed elements on earth. Many ancient peoples believed that the planet gods had to be worshipped into order to produce beneficial results for the earth.

During the first century there was an interesting connection between the sun and Rome. The religion of the Roman army—the army of the Beast to John—was the cult of Mithras. The sun god Sol Invictus played an important part in that religion. The savior figure Mithras was often depicted in religious art of this cult as slaying the cosmic bull. This was the bull of Taurus, and killing this bull symbolized the dominance of the Age of Aries over the Age of Taurus. At the time the Book of Revelation was written, the Age of Aries was ending and the age of Pisces beginning. The dominance of Aries over Taurus was soon to be history. As Aries ended, the Mithras cult gradually lost power and Christianity ascended as a major religion of the Age of Pisces. Meanwhile, Mahayana Buddhism was beginning to replace other religious traditions in India, China, and Southeast Asia, and modern Hinduism and Jainism were replacing the old Vedic traditions in India. Islam was a somewhat later development of the Age of Pisces. Christianity has been the most widespread single religion, but all of these religious traditions have flourished in their own areas during the Piscean Age.

In the first century, the religion of Mithras was seen as a major competitor of Christianity, particularly as the religion of the Roman army, since the army not only gave power to the Beast of Rome but the occupying forces of Rome were a significant presence in many lands, and retired soldiers often settled in vassal lands. We know that the Mithras cult was considered a threat to Christianity even when Christianity became more established during the next few centuries. The birthday of Mithras, December 25, was taken for the birthday of Jesus (the New Testament does not tell us when Jesus was born) and became the most widely celebrated holy day of the Piscean Age. In Christian Rome, St. Peter's Basilica, once the center of Western Christianity, was built on top of a Mithraic temple. At the time the Book of Revelation was written, however, the absorption of the Mithraic cult lay about two and a half centuries in the future, and the essence of the cult was perceived as the essence of evil.

For the early Christians, the pagan figure of Mithras and the worship of the physical sun in the form of Sol Invictus—worship of a part of creation instead of the Creator—was an example of the evil tendency of the Roman Beast to try and usurp the rightful place of God. The Mithras cult and Sol Invictus gave their satanic power to the army of the Roman Beast, emphasizing, in Christian eyes, the evil nature of this power. The number 666 was also the sum of the first six Roman numerals, I, V, X, L, C, and D, further linking 666 to Rome.

A NEW HARMONY

The numerical equivalent for the name Jesus in Greek (ΙΗΣΟΥΣ) was 888, another triple number. As we saw, the number three was very important in the Hebrew tradition and was linked to divine action, and so triple numbers had a special significance. Up to that time, the physical sun, in the form of the number 666, had been ruling the world. The number 888 was a significant harmonic change from 666. Jesus as the "light of the world" was the spiritual sun instead of the material.

In Pythagorean thought, the cosmos (creation) was made up of a dynamic harmony of opposing or opposite forces. There was night and day, summer and winter, masculine and feminine, fire and water. This fitting together of opposites was seen as a principle of *logos,* or proportion.[1]

Plato taught that harmonics are important for gaining personal harmony, or the bringing together of opposites in each individual:

The just man does not allow the several elements in his soul to usurp one another's functions; he is indeed one who sets his house in order, by self-mastery and discipline coming to be at peace with himself, and bringing into tune those three parts, like the terms in the proportion of a musical scale, the highest and the lowest notes and the means between them, will he harmonize all the intermediate intervals. Only when he has linked these parts together in well-tempered harmony and has made

himself one man instead of many, will he be ready to go about
whatever he may have to do.[2]

Plato believed in an ideal harmony set up in heaven toward which humanity could strive but never quite reach on earth. For the early Christians, Jesus was that harmony in the flesh, the high note and the low note, the first and the last, the Alpha and the Omega.

Even though humanity in general could not achieve complete harmony, humanity was still seen as the part of creation with the greatest potential for doing so. As David Fideler has written:

One of the most widespread cosmological ideas at the begin-
ning of the common era, entertained by both pagan and Chris-
tian philosophers alike, is that humanity represents the living
harmony and synthesis of all the forces which make up the cos-
mos. A child of earth and heaven, humanity is the living bridge
between matter and spirit, a living, harmonic image of the en-
tire universe.[3]

For John in the Book of Revelation, Jesus, as the Alpha and the Omega (Rev. 1:8; 21:6; 22:13), the beginning and end, the low note and the high note, is no doubt also in a harmony of intervals of all that comes between. Harmonic ratios and their role in Greek culture, therefore, are important for understanding the Book of Revelation. The word "harmonics" means a fitting together. The Pythagorean musical scale (the one we still use today) is 6: 8: 9: 12, and includes the octave 6:12. A perfect fifth is 6:9 or 8:12 = .666 × 1,000 = 666.6 (Beast). A perfect fourth is 6:8 or 9:12 = .75. A whole tone is the 8:9 ratio, between the perfect fourth and fifth, = .888 × 1,000 = 888.8 (Jesus). The shift from the worship of the sun to the worship of the son is the shift from a perfect fifth to a whole tone. The evil tendency of the sun, a part of creation, to try and usurp the place of the Creator, was a problem of disharmony. Jesus was a new harmony, so surrendered to the will of God that he was willing to die a horrible death to help humanity.

OUT OF HARMONY

The sun, or the number 666, was not inherently evil. As a part of creation, it played an important and a good part. Only when it tried to usurp God's position and take over the whole did it become evil. In Jewish legend, Satan was the most beautiful of angels, just as the sun is the most beautiful heavenly body from an earthly perspective.

A part out of balance with the whole becomes destructive. In the ancient Greek concept of harmony, one = unity, two = duality, and three = harmony. If two of the opposing forces that make up the cosmos are out of balance, they will disrupt the unity. Three brings harmony. This is reflected in both Jewish and Christian concepts of God. In Jewish thought God is one—the unity. In Christian thought, God is one, and God is also three—the Trinity. God represents both unity and harmony. Jesus is both part of the harmony and, as 888, is a whole tone in himself. He represents the mystery of unity and harmony as one.

The number 666, as a representation of the sun, is part of an opposing duality. The other part of that duality is the moon. Several opposing characteristics are attributed to these celestial bodies. The sun is often seen as masculine and the moon as feminine; the sun as active and the moon as receptive; the sun as fire and the moon as water. The sun out of harmony with the moon becomes disruptive and destructive. As the active and fire element, the sun is more destructive than the receptive, watery moon when they are out of balance.

The number associated with the moon in antiquity was 1,080. The atomic weight of silver, which is associated with the moon in the way gold is associated with the sun, is 108. The ancients believed that we take 1,080 breaths in one hour, and the Jews divided an hour into 1,080 mimims or *chalakim*.[4] The number of receptivity is 1,080. It is the numerical value of the Holy Spirit (ΤΟ ΑΓΙΟΝ ΠΝΕΥΜΑ), and the value of Mary (ΜΑΡΙΑΜ) (192) plus Jesus (ΙΜΣΟΥΣ) (888). So it is the feminine image of the Madonna and Child.[5]

To bring the sun and moon into harmony, we can add them together to create a third harmonizing influence. The sum of 1,080 and 666 is 1,746. In Greek, this was the number of the Universal Spirit (ΤΟΠΕΥΜΑ ΚΟΣΜΟΥ). It is also the grain of mustard seed (ΚΟΚΚΟΣ ΣΙΝΑΠΕΩΣ) that Jesus compares to the kingdom of heaven (Matt. 13:31; Mark 4:30–31; Luke 13:18–19). Jesus says that faith as small as a grain of mustard seed can move a mountain (Matt. 17:20) or uproot a mulberry tree and plant it in the sea (Luke 17:6).

The essence of the sun or of the number 666, then, was only evil when out of balance. When balanced by the feminine/receptive essence, when balanced by the Holy Spirit or by faith as small as a mustard seed, it can again be creative.

BALANCE IN OUR TIME

The disharmony that the first-century Christians noted and saw as evil was the aggressive "me" energy out of balance with the energy of surrender to God or to the whole of existence. That was the situation at the end of the cusp period in the shift from the Arian to the Piscean Age. Now, as we move into the Age of Aquarius, how will that change our perceptions of religion and the religions of the Piscean Age? We know that we will be asking more questions, that we will be more accepting of differences, and that we will focus more on the whole and the big picture. This is a change that has been clearly perceptible in the past fifty years of our history, the first half of the Pisces/Aquarius cusp.

At this point in time, while we are still in the cusp period in the shift from the Piscean to the Aquarian Age, the issue of the aggressive "me" energy is still very much with us. It is that energy that leads to competition, to the desire to be the best and the first, to the desire to control others. It is the "sun" energy out of balance that leads to war, to the destruction of the environment, to totalitarianism, to imperialism, to greed. It is this energy that leads to many of the events described by various prophets for the Apocalypse.

The idea that 666 in the Book of Revelation is about Satan as a bestial creature is really a product of much later Christian demonology. When Christianity penetrated into Europe it tried to absorb the local religions. One of the deities of northern Europe was a horned god, often in the form of a goat. This god became associated with Satan, who then evolved into the image of a red devil, with a pointed tail, pointed ears, and a trident in his hand. Some people imagine that the number 666 is associated with this idea of a devil. We must be very careful not to read later ideas back into ancient times. The ancients spoke of Satan as a dragon and a serpent, but as we have seen, when they did that they were speaking mythically, not literally. The myths of dragons and serpents representing what is destructive to life were found all through Middle Eastern culture, and people could use these images to effectively communicate the idea of anti-life energy. No one in antiquity would have thought this meant that Satan was literally a dragon or a serpent.

In the same way, the energy of the beast, the nature, or 666 is a human quality, not a quality contained in an outer demon. An effort to usurp the place of God or to fight as a part against the whole is always destructive. It becomes more than that: It becomes satanic or demonic when it is carried to an extreme. The harmonic energy of Jesus, the energy of surrender to God's will or the will of the whole, balances this destructive quality. The quality of surrender is also a human quality. It becomes a divine quality when it becomes total surrender.

So when we look for the Beast, we don't have to watch for something that looks demonic on the surface. We have to watch for a human quality that becomes demonic in extreme imbalance.

LOGOS

The Greek word *logos* literally means "word," "thought," "principle," or "speech," but in classical Greek thought it had two expanded meanings. One meaning for logos was the kind of human reason that seeks universal understanding and harmony. The other meaning was a kind of universal intelligence that controls and rules the cosmos.

As far as we know, the first person to use Logos to mean universal intelligence was the Greek philosopher Heraclitus (c. 535 B.C.E.). He spoke of a rational divine intelligence that is sometimes called the mind of God. The Stoics tried to bring their lives into alignment with the Logos, or divine plan. They believed that true happiness and freedom could only be achieved that way.

In the Septuagint, or Greek translation of the Old Testament, the term "Logos" (Hebrew *davar*) was used frequently to describe God's words (Gen. 1:3, 6, 9; 3:9, 11; Ps. 32:9), God's action (Zech. 5:1–4; Ps. 106:20, 147:15), and messages of prophets by means of which God communicated his will to his people (Jer. 1:4–19, 2:1–7; Ezek. 1:3; Amos 3:1). Logos is used here only as a figure of speech referring to God's activity or action. In what is called the Jewish wisdom literature, there are also depictions of Wisdom (*hokhmah* in Hebrew and *sophia* in Greek), which can be seen as a separate personification or individualization of God. This Wisdom was active in the world as the Logos. The Torah, as the Word of God, preceded creation.

The Jewish philosopher Philo (20 B.C.E.–50 C.E.) combined these ideas in his writings, so that his Logos resembles both the Stoic will of the universal and the Hebrew Word of God. Philo, a Hellenized Jew, was trying to reconcile the Hebrew concept of a personal God with the Greek philosophical concept. Philo interpreted the Logos, which he saw as the Divine Mind, as the Platonic Form of Forms, the Idea of Ideas, or the sum total of Forms or Ideas. The Logos was an indestructible Form of Wisdom. Philo reasoned that by analogy to the biblical version of the creation of man in the image of God, so the visible world as such must have been created in the image of its archetype present in the mind of God. The writings of Philo were not preserved by Jews, but were preserved by the early Christian Church, since they provided a basis for the later Christian understanding of Jesus as the Logos.

The word *"Logos"* is found in the New Testament, which was written in Greek, and the most famous use is in John 1:1, "In the beginning was the Word [Logos], and the Word [Logos] was with God, and the Word [Logos] was God." A few passages later, the Logos becomes flesh in the form of Jesus (John 1:14). Jesus in the flesh is the bridge between the human and the divine. This also links the scriptures as the Word of God to the revelation of Jesus, as the Word incarnate.

For the Christians, an incarnation of the whole had come to replace the part of creation represented by the sun. Jesus is both surrendered to the will of the Father and is one with the Father. He is the Creator and the creation, the beginning and the end, the Alpha and the Omega. He is the link between multiplicity and unity.

CHAPTER 8

APOCALYPSE

Apocalyptic predictions throughout the Bible tell us that before the End Time, which will be followed by the coming of the Messiah, there will be a period of devastating events. This prediction is not for the end of the world but for the end of the time before the Messiah takes control of the earth. Predictions include war; famine; pestilence and disease; environmental damage; dramatic earth changes, such as earthquakes, volcanic eruptions, and a possible pole shift of the planet; the death of millions of people; and various cosmic events, such as comets and eclipses.

There have been several historical periods of devastating destruction for the Hebrew people featured in the Old Testament. At the time of Assyrian invasions and the Babylonian captivity, the majority of the tribes of Israel were lost, many people were killed, the Temple was destroyed, the sacred vessels stolen, the land devastated, and a small remnant of the people was held in captivity for two generations.

After a miraculous and unexpected defeat of Babylon, the Hebrew people were freed and returned to Jerusalem to rebuild the Temple. In the first century, they rebelled against Rome and were defeated. Many were killed, Jerusalem was sacked, the Temple was destroyed, and the Hebrew people were sent into a diaspora throughout the world.

The Jews who settled in Europe suffered hundreds of years of persecution, including banishment, forced conversion, restriction to ghettos, and pogroms at the hands of the European Christian nations, which blamed the Jews for the crucifixion of Christ. This culminated in the twentieth century in the Holocaust of World War II, during which millions of Jews were herded into concentration camps, transported in cattle cars in which many died, and gassed in large groups. The structure of Jewish culture in much of Europe was destroyed.

Three years after the end of World War II, in 1948, the nation of Israel was reestablished, and many Jews began returning to Israel. This caused understandable concern to the people who were already living there, and hostilities broke out. Israel fought a war in 1948 to preserve its right to exist. In 1967, Israel was attacked by an alliance of Arab nations, which refused to accept the existence of Israel. In a seemingly miraculous series of events, Israel won that war and the survival of Israel ceased to be a question. Instead of the devastating conflict that was expected, the war was over in six days. Israel's relationship with the Palestinians who had occupied the land for generations is still not resolved, but the survival of Israel is no longer the issue.

Some interpreters of Biblical prophecy argue that the events of antiquity already demonstrate a fulfillment of prophecy. The Hebrew people were devastated, taken captive, and returned to rebuild the Temple. This, some people argue, fulfilled Old Testament prophecies. Then Jesus said that the Temple would be destroyed in three days. He also predicted devastation for Jews and said this would happen within his own generation. In 70 C.E., approximately forty years after the death of Jesus, Jerusalem was devastated, the

Temple was destroyed, and the Jewish people fled. So was the prediction fulfilled?

The answer to that depends on whether one interprets the New Testament prophecies to mean that the destruction of the Temple and the End Time will happen at the same time, as we will discuss in chapter 10. The most common interpretation is that the rise of a beast-nation and an Antichrist and apocalyptic events will happen again just before the Messiah comes, but the Temple in Jerusalem will not be rebuilt before the return.

For our purposes here, we will assume that the prophecies were fulfilled to some extent in the first century, but we will look to see if there has been further fulfillment since then. As we saw in the last two chapters, there have been at least three series of beast-nations and Antichrist figures that we can identify: Babylon and Nebuchadnezzar, Rome and Nero, and Nazi Germany and Adolph Hitler.

TWENTIETH-CENTURY APOCALYPSE

Did the presence of those satanic figures on the earth coincide with an apocalyptic period? We don't have much information about the time of the Babylonian captivity, but we do know that there was so much apocalyptic activity during the first century that there was a widespread belief that the End Time was at hand. Halley's Comet appeared around 60 C.E., and according to the historian Josephus, "hung like a sword in the sky." Some said it presaged the death of Nero, who killed himself by stabbing himself in the throat in 68. The comet reappeared in 64, and Nero was so disturbed by it that he ordered dozens of nobles executed.[1] That was also the year of the terrible fire that destroyed much of Rome. Christians were blamed for it, and many were slaughtered. In 70, Jerusalem and the Temple were destroyed and the nation of Israel sent into exile. In 79, Mount Vesuvius, the volcano south of Rome, erupted, filling the sky with dust and blocking the sun and moon over a large area. The cloud of dust must have reminded the people of the Middle East of the scirocco, or "breath of God." This is a form of windstorm that fills the sky with sand and gives the sun and moon a blood-red cast. It sometimes drives waves of locusts into the land, where they destroy all crops. Clouds of locusts are so large that they can darken the sky and wipe out plants, leading to famine and pestilence.[2] These events, plus large-scale warfare that resulted in famine and disease, convinced many in the first century that the end was near.

In the 1930s, a new beast-nation and new Antichrist figure arose and started a war that included the entire planet. There were battlefronts in Europe, Eastern Europe, the Middle East, Asia and East Asia, and the Pacific. The American continent was not a battleground, but millions came from there to fight in other places. Did apocalyptic events occur at this time?

Because the first-century expectations of the end were not fulfilled, many people are hesitant to believe that some kind of end or major change will come in our time. They are also hesitant to identify events as apocalyptic. We have become so inured to horror that we do not recognize it for what it is. We see the kind of scenes that awed and probably terrified the biblical prophets, nightly on our television screens. We see bombings, war, murder, mutilated bodies, and a wide variety of human suffering and ecological disaster so often that we usually just shut them out.

If we take a step back from this overload of horror and take an objective look at the last century, we will see that the twentieth century was filled with apocalyptic events, including war, genocide, ecological disaster, incurable disease, earthquakes, volcanic eruptions, and cosmic events. We have become so used to these disasters that we assume the biblical apocalypse will be even worse. But will it?

Let's look more closely at the events of the twentieth century. The early part of the century was marked by rebellions against the old imperialistic order of European world domination and empires such as that of the Ottoman Turks. The century marked the end of the European empires around the world, and the establishment of European and American economic domination instead. The century started with rebellions in Africa, the Middle East, China, and Portugal. The Balkan War began in 1912, and World War I only two years later. That was a conflict that embroiled most of Europe and much of the Middle East; millions died in mud- and blood-filled trenches. Chemical warfare in the form of toxic gases was used for the first time in a major conflict.

This was followed by the Communist revolution in Russia, in which millions died. Meanwhile, Germany, struggling to recover from World War I and the sanctions imposed in retribution for it, fell prey to the influences of the Nazi party. The first concentration camps, in which millions of people would die, were set up in 1933. Three years later, Hitler received 99 percent of the vote in a German election, in a nation deceived by a truly satanic power. During the course of the war, bombs were used extensively in London, Germany, the Pacific, and eventually Japan, resulting in widespread devastation and millions of deaths.

After that war, the Cold War period began in which the US and the USSR fought a propaganda war and armed other countries for local warfare. It is estimated that more than 66 million people died in World War II but that more than that number died in a series of smaller wars that continued for the rest of the century. Those include the Korean War, the Vietnam War that France, the US, and other forces fought in Vietnam and other areas of Southeast Asia, and conflicts in Bosnia and other areas of Eastern Europe that erupted after the breakup of the USSR. They also include the Chinese occupation of Tibet and ongoing conflict between India and Pakistan, Pakistan and Afghanistan, Russia and Afghanistan, and conflicts among various nations in Africa and the Middle East. Estimates for war-related deaths during the century reach as high as 200 million.[3]

Several of these conflicts have included genocide and atrocities similar to the European holocaust. The Pol Pot regime in Cambodia slaughtered millions. Mass graves of up to three million people were found when the regime was ousted. The Chinese settlement of Tibet resulted in the sacking of Buddhist temples and widespread slaughter. Millions more died or were imprisoned during the Chinese Cultural Revolution. The Bosnian conflict included an attempt at "ethnic cleansing" in the slaughter of Muslim residents. The twentieth century also marked an escalation of terrorism, from plane hijacking to bombing, from Ireland, to the Middle East, to Oklahoma City.

And war and terrorism were not the only apocalyptic events of the twentieth century. Of the ten deadliest earthquakes in recorded history, six occurred in the twentieth century. In 1908, 100,000 people died in Italy, 200,000 in China in 1920, 143,000 in Japan in 1923, 200,000 in China in 1927, 110,000 in Turkmenistan in 1948, and 255,000 in China in 1976.[4] A major insurance company estimated that there were an average of 1.5 million deaths per century from natural disasters such as floods, earthquakes, and volcanoes for most of the second millennium, but there were 3.5 million deaths from those causes in the twentieth century alone.[5] One of the largest known volcanic eruptions, the eruption of Mt. Saint

Helens, happened in May 1980 in the state of Washington. Few people were killed in the remote area, but billions of dollars of damage was estimated, dust and smoke particles covered a several-state radius, and trees in a five-mile radius were blasted flat by the shock waves.

Famines also occurred around the world, including those in Biafra, Africa, Tibet, and Afghanistan. Estimates on the number of deaths by famine range from forty-four to seventy million. Incurable disease killed millions. Cancer became the leading cause of death in many developed areas of the world, and AIDS killed over 950 million people in the last two decades of the century.

In addition to war, natural disaster, and disease, we have experienced a series of environmental disasters, the likes of which humanity has never seen before. These include oil spills, air pollution, acid rain, water pollution, ozone layer depletion, depletion of oxygen-producing forests, and global warming.

We have experienced all these horrors, yet we are expecting worse to come. This is partly because the images of apocalyptic prophecy have not been fulfilled exactly. We have not seen locusts with human faces or the sun and moon falling. It is important to remember that the biblical prophecies were based on events seen in visions by ancient people who had no concept of machines or technology. They described the events they saw in the only terms they understood. Here are some apocalyptic prophecies from the Bible that may have been fulfilled in the twentieth century:

> *Immediately after the tribulation of those days shall the sun be darkened, and the moon shall not give her light, and the stars shall fall from heaven, and the powers of the heavens shall be shaken (Matt. 24:29).*

At the end of World War II, two of the newly developed atomic bombs were dropped on Japan. The Hiroshima mission, planned to bring the Japanese "to heel," was flawlessly executed. The bomb was dropped exactly at the intended aiming point, and because Hiroshima is built on a flat river delta, the relatively small bomb— known as "Little Boy"—with an explosive force of only twelve kilotons, did maximum damage. The "Fat Man" bomb devastated the western part of Nagasaki a few days later.

The blast at Hiroshima, with an intensity greater than that of the sun, blinded three hundred thousand people in an instant, and a blast-generated wind knocked them down and tore the clothing from their bodies. Some were vaporized. This was followed by five minutes of deadly black radioactive rain that vaporized on hitting the ground:

And the name of the star is called Wormwood: and the third part of the waters became wormwood; and many men died of the waters, because they were made bitter (Rev. 8:11).

On April 26, 1986, explosions destroyed the nuclear reactor at the power station in Chernobyl. Radioactive material was blasted high into the air and then settled back down to pollute air and water as far away as Japan, China, the US, and Canada. High levels of radiation were recorded throughout Europe. However, it is estimated that 70 percent of the radiation fell back on the country of Belarus, where Chernobyl is located. Almost one quarter of the country is contaminated and agriculture has been forbidden in some areas. The Ukrainian word for wormwood is Chernobyl.[6]

During the Vietnam War, millions of gallons of Agent Orange, a herbicide contaminated with dioxin, was air-dropped on Vietnam by the US military in white clouds. It saturated the land and the water. Dioxin has since been linked with several kinds of cancer, skin disease, birth defects, infertility, stillbirths and spontaneous abortions, and childhood cancer in offspring.[7] The Red Cross estimates that one million people in Vietnam are suffering serious health problems over twenty-five years after the end of the war because of dioxin contamination.[8]

The battlefield of the Gulf War has been called a toxic field, with exposure to the nerve gas sarin, cyclosarin, and mustard gas. Seven hundred oil wells were set on fire, sending incredible amounts of pollution into the atmosphere.

APOCALYPSE NOW

Looking back on the twentieth century, it is clear that it was an apocalyptic time. Does humanity have to experience another and even more devastating Apocalypse before the Messiah comes? Or is there a possibility that the Messiah can return right now?

CHAPTER 9

GOG AND MAGOG IN THE BATTLE OF ARMAGEDDON

According to the Book of Revelation, the last battle before the coming of the Messiah will be at Armageddon. It is spelled Harmagedon in the New Revised Standard Version of the Bible. Scholars generally consider Armageddon or Harmagedon to be a transliteration of the Hebrew *har megiddo*, or mountain of Megiddo. Megiddo is a town located in the Jezreel Valley. This valley is located about halfway between Haifa, on the Mediterranean coast, and Tiberias, on the Sea of Galilee. Some scholars object to this explanation for Armageddon, since there is no mountain there. There is, however, a tell or hill that rises about seventy feet above the plain, which would probably be enough to explain why the city would be known to some as *har megiddo* in the first century.

We are going to discuss who Gog and Magog might be in this chapter on Armageddon, because Ezekiel, and writers like Hal Lindsey, have placed Gog and Magog in the battle of Armageddon. The Book of Revelation, as we will see, puts Gog and Magog at the final battle, at the end of the world, not at the battle of Armageddon. Since that final battle is to take place after the Millennium of peace that happens after the Messiah returns, it would be hard to speculate what the world might look like at that time. It will only be useful to identify Gog and Magog if they are involved at the battle of Armageddon.

The theme of a great battle between good and evil—with Israel representing good and the enemies of Israel representing evil—that is to take place before God takes over control of the world through the Messiah, runs through the Old Testament. In Daniel 7:3–7, the evil beast representing a kingdom of Israel's enemies rises up from the water and destroys what is around it with its iron teeth and feet. This beast is then destroyed by God, and dominion over the earth is given to the Messiah. There is no mention of Armageddon, Megiddo, or Gog and Magog.

In Ezekiel 38, Gog, the prince of Magog, Meshech, and Tubal and hordes of his allies will invade Israel and be defeated by God. Lindsey identifies this battle as the battle of Armageddon, but not everyone agrees. In the Book of Revelation 16:12–16, the battle of Armageddon is fought when the spirits of Satan, the beast-nation, and the Antichrist travel over all the nations and assemble them for battle. Gog and Magog do not enter into the picture until after the Millennium of peace (Rev. 20:7–10), when Satan deceives them and they rise up against God. This is the last battle before Judgment Day. In Zechariah 12:3, the hordes against Israel come from all the nations of the earth.

This inconsistency and inexactness should caution us against taking Ezekiel 38 too literally, as Lindsey and others have done. Since the other biblical predictions say that the invaders in this battle will come from all the nations, the list in Ezekiel may well be a symbolic list of historical enemies of Israel and not an indicator of specific people who will be involved in the battle. On the other hand, all the nations may refer to the list in Ezekiel, so we will look closely at the information we have to identify these people.

ARMAGEDDON

The name Armageddon doesn't appear anywhere in the Bible except in Revelation 16:16. Megiddo, however, does appear in Zechariah 12:10–11.

> *And I will pour upon the house of David, and upon the inhabitants of Jerusalem, the spirit of grace and of supplications: and they shall look upon me whom they have pierced, and they shall mourn for him, as one mourneth for his only son, and shall be in bitterness for him, as one that is in bitterness for his firstborn. In that day shall there be a great mourning in Jerusalem, as the mourning of Hadadrimmon in the valley of Megiddon.*

Zechariah was a prophet from about the sixth century B.C.E., whose prophecies resemble those of the Book of Revelation. Zechariah summarized the earlier prophecies of Joel, Isaiah, Ezekiel, and Daniel, in much the same way that John summarized the prophecies of Jesus (Matt. 24, Mark 13, Luke 21) and Paul (I Thess. 5, II Thess. 2). John, the writer of Revelation, may have gotten the idea that the last battle would happen in Meggido from this reference in Zechariah. This is particularly likely, since Zechariah mentions Megiddo in the context of the last great battle of the people of Israel before the Messiah comes. Though Zechariah does not place the battle at Megiddo, the parallel is very strong.

There was another reason why the battle might happen at Megiddo: the last free king (not a puppet of an outside power) from the House of David was killed there in battle. The king was Josiah—considered by some to be a second king David. He was killed in a battle with Pharaoh Necho II of Egypt in 609 B.C.E.

Since the last real king of the House of David died at Megiddo, what better place for the Kingdom of God to return in the form of the Davidic Messiah?

Megiddo is located at a crossroads for people in the area who are moving north or south, and probably as a result of that it has been more blood-soaked than almost any place on the planet. The first battle of recorded history, between Thutmose III of Egypt and the Canaanites, was fought there in about 1479 B.C.E. We know of at least thirty-four bloody battles that have been fought in the small area of Megiddo and the Jezreel Valley, and there may have been more in ancient times. Egyptians, Canaanites, Israelites, Midianites, Amalekites, Philistines, Hasmoneans, Greeks, Romans, Byzantines, Muslims, Crusaders, Mamlukes, Mongols, Palestinians, French, Ottomans, British, Australians, Germans, Arabs, and Israelis have fought and died there.[1]

It is interesting to note that at the time John wrote the Book of Revelation, only thirteen of the battles we know about had been fought there. Since the time that Revelation was written, there have been fourteen more major battles, several in modern times. The last great battle that had been fought there in John's time was the battle between the Roman emperor Vespasian and the Jewish rebels in 67 C.E., shortly before Titus destroyed Jerusalem in 70. Vespasian had defeated the rebels, which may have been another wrong to be righted by God from John's point of view.

In the tenth century, the Jezreel Valley was the site of battles between Byzantine and Islamic forces. In the twelfth and thirteenth centuries, Christians came in two waves from Europe to fight the Islamic occupants. The Crusaders came first, and were followed by the Hospitallers and Templars. At the end of the eighteenth century, Napoleon fought the Turks there, and during World War I British troops defeated the Turks, eventually taking control of Palestine.

There have been several battles there since the restoration of Israel. Israel fought Arab forces there in two battles in 1948 and again in the famous Six Day War of 1967. There was an additional battle against Syria in 1973.

Given the reference to Megiddo in Zechariah, it is possible that the mention of Armageddon in Revelation is only symbolic—a reference back to Zechariah. As we have seen, several prophets mention a battle like the one described in Revelation, but none of the others gives a location for it. On the other hand, given the number of battles that have already been fought at Megiddo, it is equally possible that this will be the location of a great battle as predicted. It is also possible that the battle has already taken place since the restoration of Israel.

THE BATTLE

What is this battle supposed to be? There is a lot of confusion about that question. Some people seem to think that Armageddon is the battle at the end of the world, but in the Book of Revelation it is the battle before the Messiah comes. As we said, the final battle between Gog and Magog and the forces of good takes place in the Book of Revelation after the Millennium of peace under the leadership of the Messiah and resurrected saints.

There is also a tendency among interpreters to describe Armageddon as though it includes all the disasters of the Apocalypse.[2] However, John and other prophetic writers like Zechariah describe this battle as a simple battle in which a huge army will come against Israel and be defeated by the intervention of God. After this battle, the Messiah will come. Most interpreters assume that the Messiah will come immediately in the midst of this battle, but since we know that biblical time is often symbolic and, therefore, extremely inexact, it may well be that the Messiah will not return for several years after the battle.

GOG AND MAGOG

Who will the army be that invades Israel? We saw that the prophets do not describe the enemy of Israel in the same way, and that Ezekiel is the most specific. He writes that the invasion of Israel will be made by a great northern enemy and others:

> The word of the LORD came to me: "Son of man, set your face against Gog, of the land of Magog, the chief prince of Meshech and Tubal; prophesy against him and say: 'This is what the Sovereign LORD says: I am against you, O Gog, chief prince of Meshech and Tubal. I will turn you around, put hooks in your jaws and bring you out with your whole army—your horses, your horsemen fully armed, and a great horde with large and small shields, all of them brandishing their swords. Persia, Cush and Put will be with them, all with shields and helmets, also Gomer with all its troops, and Beth Togarmah from the far north with all its troops—the many nations with you" (Ezek. 38:1–6, NIV translation).

In 1968, Richard W. DeHaan published a book, *Israel and the Nations in Prophecy,* in which he used eighteenth- and nineteenth-century sources to tie Gog and Magog to Russia. The idea was picked up and expanded by Hal Lindsey in his massively best-selling book *The Late Great Planet Earth.* Lindsay ignored the prophecy in Revelation that said Gog and Magog would fight the final battle and not the battle of Armageddon, and relied completely on an interpretation of Ezekiel.

Like DeHaan, Lindsey used old, obscure, and academically unsound sources to support his theory. A nineteenth-century medical doctor named John Cummings was one of his primary sources, from a book written in 1864. Another source was an obscure and very questionable Hebrew lexicon written in the early 1800s. Using very contorted logic, Lindsey made the Hebrew word *rosh*, meaning prince, into a proper name and linked it to Russia through the Byzantine and Arabic names Rōs and Rūs. Meshech, from Ezekiel, became Moscow, and Tubal became a tribe in Russia. Persia was identified as Iran, Ethiopia or Cush as Black Africa, Put as the Arab nations, and Gomer as the Eastern European nations of the Russian Bloc. In this way, Lindsey managed to appeal to both Cold War and racial fears, and sold a lot of books.

Since that time, however, communism has declined radically and the USSR has been disbanded. Lindsey's interpretations no longer look so believable. Reputable modern scholars have also completely rejected his theories about the meanings of *rosh*, Meshech, and Tubal.

Many of the names in Ezekiel 38 first appear in Genesis 10:1–7:

Now these are the generations of the sons of Noah, Shem, Ham, and Japheth: and unto them were sons born after the flood.

The sons of Japheth; Gomer, and Magog, and Madai, and Javan, and Tubal, and Meshech, and Tiras. And the sons of Gomer; Ashkenaz, and Riphath, and Togarmah. And the sons of Javan; Elishah, and Tarshish, Kittim, and Dodanim. By these were the isles of the Gentiles divided in their lands; every one after his tongue, after their families, in their nations.

And the sons of Ham; Cush, and Mizraim, and Phut,

and Canaan. And the sons of Cush; Seba, and Havilah, and
Sabtah, and Raamah, and Sabtechah: and the sons of Raamah;
Sheba, and Dedan.

This section of Genesis is a description of the descendants of Noah who repopulated the earth after the great flood. Gomer, Magog, Tubal, and Meshech are all listed as descendants of Noah's son Japeth. Cush and Put are the descendants of Ham, whose descendants also included the Canaanites. Ham was the accursed son of Noah, because he had seen his father's nakedness and had done something not specified to Noah (Gen. 9:20–27).

All of these descendants appear to have settled in the Middle East or adjacent lands. The descendants of Noah represented all of the nations of the world as it appeared to the ancient writers. Because all other people had drowned in the flood, the descendants of Noah were the peoples of the world. Ezekiel's list of so many of the descendants of Noah was probably intended as a symbolic representation of the "all the nations" of the other biblical prophets. At the very least, he was saying that most of the people from their known world would rise up and attack Israel.

Genesis moves from the description of the descendants of Noah to the story of the settlement in the land of Shinar, where the tower of Babel is built (Gen. 11:1–9). Shinar is identified in Daniel 1:1–2 as Babylon. For Ezekiel 38, then, the tribes may also have symbolized Babylon and its vassals. Babylon would fall and Israel would be rebuilt, but these ancient enemies would rise against Israel one last time before they were destroyed forever. As we have seen many times, Babylon is used in post-exile Jewish prophecy to symbolize all that is evil and satanic in the world.

Modern scholars have a different or additional theory about the origin of the names in Ezekiel. The names *Mushki* and *Tabali* may be forms of Meshech and Tubal. They are connected to one of the greatest of the early kings of Assyria, Tiglath-pileser (reigned c. 1115–c. 1077 B.C.E.), who ascended the throne at the time when a people known as the Mushki, or Mushku, probably Phrygians, were pushing into Asia Minor. Phrygia was located in what is now western Turkey. The invasion of the Mushki constituted a serious threat to Middle Eastern civilization, because Asia Minor was the principal source of iron, which was then coming into general use. Tiglath-pileser defeated 20,000 Mushki in the Assyrian province of Kummukh (Commagene). He also defeated the Nairi, who lived west of Lake Van, extending Assyrian control farther into Asia Minor than any of his predecessors had done.

From this we see that Gog and Magog, connected in Ezekiel 38 with Meshech and Tubal, may be either a symbolic reference to barbarian tribes or a specific reference to the ancient Mushki, who probably came from what is now Turkey or an area adjacent to there, such as modern Georgia, Armenia, or the northern areas of Iran and Iraq. This may be the area far in the north that Ezekiel speaks of. These areas are all considerably north of Israel, and may have been the home of some of the most northern people that the ancient Hebrews dealt with at that time. Even if they knew that people lived north of there, it is unlikely that the Hebrews would have expected armies to come from farther away. So modern Turkey and neighboring countries may have been Ezekiel's concept of the extreme north.

It is fascinating to note that an interpretation of end time prophecies in the Qur'an also place Gog and Magog in the area east of Turkey. The religion of Islam arose from Judaism, as Christianity did, and the prophecies in the Qur'an, the prophecies of the great Islamic prophet Mohammed, include many prophecies similar to those of the Old Testament or Hebrew Bible.

The first reference to Gog and Magog is found in *Surah* (chapter) 18, *Al Kahf* (The Cave):

They will ask you of Dhu al Qarnayan. Say: I shall recite unto you a (true) account of him. Lo! We made him strong in the land and gave him unto everything in a road. And he followed a road. Till, when he reached the setting place of the sun, he found it setting in a muddy spring, and found a people thereabout: We said: O Dhul al Qarnayn! Either punish or show them kindness. He said: As for him who does wrong, we shall punish him, and then he will be brought back unto his Lord, who will punish him with awful punishment! Bus as for him who believes and does right, good will be his reward, and We shall speak unto him a mild command. Then he followed a road. Till, when he reached the rising place of the sun, he found it rising on a people for whom We had appointed no shelter therefrom. So (it was). And We knew all concerning him. Then he followed a road. Till, when he came between the two mountains, he found upon their hither side a folk that scarce could understand a saying. They said: O Duh al Qarnayn! Lo! Gog and Magog are spoiling the land. So may we pay you tribute on condition that you set a barrier between us and them? He said: That wherein my Lord has established me is better (than you tribute). Do but help me with strength (of men), I will set between you and them a bank. Give me chains of iron till, when he had leveled up (the gap) between the cliffs, he said: Blow! till, when he had made it a fire, he said: Bring me molten copper to pour thereon. And (Gog and Magog) were not able to surmount, nor could they pierce (it). He said: This is a mercy from my Lord; but when the promise of my Lord comes to pass, He will crush it, for the promise of my Lord is true.

And on that day We shall let some of them surge against others, and the Trumpet will be blown. Then We shall gather them together in one gathering. On that day we shall present Hell to disbelievers, plain to view (Q 18:83–100).[3]

The second reference to Gog and Magog in the Qur'an, which places Gog and Magog in the battle just before the Final Judgment, is from *Surah* 21, *Al Anbiya* (The Prophets):

Lo! this, your religion, is one religion, and I am your Lord, so worship Me. And they have broken their religion (into fragments) among them (yet) all are returning unto Us. Then who does good works and is a believer, there will be no rejection of his effort. Lo! We record (it) for him. And there is a ban upon any community which We have destroyed: that they shall not return. Until, when Gog and Magog are let loose, and they hasten out of every mound. And the True Promise draws near; then behold them, staring wide (in terror), the eyes of those who disbelieve! (They say): Alas for us! We (lived) in forgetfulness of this. Ah, but we were wrongdoers! Lo! you (idolaters) and that which you worship beside Allah are fuel of Hell. Thereunto you will come. If these had been Gods they would not have come thither, but all will abide therein. Therein wailing is their portion, and therein they hear not. Lo! those unto whom kindness has gone forth before from Us, they will be far removed from there. They will not hear the slightest sound thereof, while they abide in that which their souls desire (Q 21:92–102).

According to Islamic interpreters, Dhu-al-Qarnain (or Duh al Qarnayn) means "the two horned one" or "one whose rule extends over two generations" or "the lord of two kingdoms." In Daniel

8:20, the angel Gabriel interprets part of Daniel's vision, saying that the ram with two horns in the vision means the king of Media and Persia. From this, some Islamic interpreters have concluded that Duh al Qarnayn was a king of the Persian Empire who traveled widely and conquered other nations. The one who fits that description is Darius I.

Darius was the ruler of the Persian Empire from 522 to 486. Darius is not to be confused with two later Persian kings, Darius II (423–404 B.C.E.) and Darius the III (336–330 B.C.E.) He was a cousin of Cambyses and Smerdis, the sons of Cyrus the Great, the founder of the Persian empire and the general who defeated Babylon. After Cambyses committed suicide, Smerdis or an impostor ruled the empire. Darius participated in an attempt to kill Smerdis or the impostor, and in the process he managed to usurp the throne.

He expanded the Persian Empire to its greatest extent, conquering the Indus Valley, the southeastern corner of Europe, and part of Libya. He was best known for his administrative skills, because he developed a system of government that divided the empire into twenty satrapies, with administrators, or satraps, to govern them. He also kept a group of expert advisers who could be sent into the satrapies when needed. He developed coinage and organized tributes to the government and local military forces in each satrapy.

About 512, Darius undertook a war against the Scythians (part of modern Turkey). A great army conquered an area of northern Greece, and crossed the Danube in modern Bulgaria, heading east, close to the Black Sea. The expedition seems to have been based on faulty geographical information: Having advanced for some weeks into the Russian steppes, Darius was forced to return.

Darius left many inscriptions, which give us an unusual amount of information about him. He appears to have been a Zoroastrian who claimed an intimate relationship with the god Ahuramazda. In that sense, he was a monotheist, but he tolerated the religions of his subject people, including the religion of the Hebrews.

The location for the Qur-anic story about Gog and Magog and the two-horned leader depends on a different translation for Qur'an 18:86 than the one we have used here. The translation we have used says, "Till, when he reached the setting place of the sun, he found it setting in a muddy spring." Other translations say, "Until when he reached the setting place of the sun [or the westernmost point], he found it going down into a black sea." The Black Sea translation makes more sense, since this place would not appear to be the setting place of the sun, unless it was the westernmost point of land before some large body of water. From the "black sea" translation, Islamic interpreters place the western border for this event on the east coast of the Black Sea, which today would be Georgia or Turkey.

The Qur'an 18:93 in both translations talks about a place between two mountains where people speak another language. Interpreters place this in the mountains of Armenia and Azerbaijan. The wall is identified as the famous wall of Derbent (or Darband).

This wall is to be found on the shore of the Caspian Sea. There is a mention of it in *Marasid al-Ittila*, a famous book of geography. Ibn al-Faqih also mentions it in his book. The *Encyclopaedia Biblica* gives the following account of the wall:

> *Derbent or Darband, a town of Persia, Causcasia, in the province of Daghistan, on the Western shore of the Caspian . . . to the south lies the seaward extremity of the Caucasian wall, 50 miles long otherwise known as Alexander's Wall . . . This, when entire, had a height of 29 ft. and a thickness of about 10 ft. and with its iron gates and numerous watchtowers formed a valuable defense of the Persian frontier.[4]*

Islamic interpreters do not all agree on the identity of Gog and Magog, but there are some interesting points in their theories. Ibn Kathir writes that they are descendants of Adam, and this view is supported by the *hadith,* or stories about the Prophet, in *Muslim* and *Bukhari.* According to Ruh al-Ma'ani, they are two tribes from among the descendants of Noah's son Japeth, of whom the Turks form a part, being so called because they were left (turiku) on the other side of the wall. Moreover, the Qur'an's own description shows clearly that they are human beings, and that the wall was constructed to ward off their invasion.[5]

So both modern Western interpretations of Ezekiel and Islamic interpretations of the Qur'an place Gog and Magog in or near the areas of Turkey, Georgia, Armenia, Azerbaijan, and northern areas of Iran and Iraq. Some of the other names in Ezekiel are easy to identify. Put was widely used for an area including, but larger than, modern Libya. Cush was an area of Africa south of Egypt. These are such common meanings that the King James translation uses Ethiopia and Libya, instead of Cush and Put. Genesis tells us that the other names mentioned in Ezekiel are the names of people who settled throughout the Middle East, which was the whole world as the ancient Hebrews knew it.

ARMAGEDDON IN 1967?

In 1967, Israel fought the Six Day War against the allied forces of Egypt, Syria, Jordan, and Iraq, who were armed with weapons supplied by the USSR, far to the north. A major battle of that war was fought in Megiddo on June 5 and 6. Against all odds, Israel was spectacularly successful, scoring a victory in six days that shocked the world and established Israel as a nation that would survive.

Most interpreters of End Time prophecies, including Lindsey, agree that this war was a significant event.

The battle fought in Megiddo during the Six Day War has not been identified as the battle of Armageddon because of a belief that the end of that battle will be magical or supernatural, with the Messiah literally coming to earth on a cloud. As we will see, many biblical prophecies have been fulfilled in amazing ways but none have been fulfilled magically or supernaturally. In every case, God has used humans as agents to fulfill his wishes. In the Book of Revelation, we have an indication that this is still the case. The battle of Armageddon is to be fought by humans who were inspired by the spirit of Satan. The final battle with Gog and Magog is to be fought by humans deceived by Satan.

The nearly miraculous result of the Six Day War may well have been the battle of Armageddon that foretells the coming of the Messiah in our time.

CHAPTER 10

ISRAEL AND THE TEMPLE

The question of whether the Temple in Jerusalem must be physically rebuilt before the Messiah returns is a subject hotly debated by both Jews and Christians. The difficulty is that the Islamic Dome of the Rock is situated where the first two Jewish Temples were located. A new Temple could not be built unless the Dome of the Rock was removed by a natural disaster or human agency. An attempt to remove the building would guarantee a major war. Does the Dome of the Rock have to be removed and the Jewish Temple rebuilt on the spot before the Messiah can return?

THE TEMPLE MOUNT AND SOLOMON'S TEMPLE

The location of the two Jewish Temples has a fascinating history. The earliest traces of settlement in the area date back to 3000 B.C.E., and archaeological evidence shows that the settlement there was called Urusalim, meaning "Foundation of God." In about 1000 B.C.E., the Hebrew king David, who united the kingdoms of Israel and Judea, conquered the city. He renamed it Jerusalem, "City of

Peace." It became the capital of the new kingdom, and in about 955, the sacred Ark of the Covenant was brought there. David chose Mt. Moriah as the site of the Temple that was to be built to house the Ark.

King Solomon was King David's son. The Bible tells us that King David wanted to build the first Temple, but the prophet Nathan said that God did not agree. God decreed that Solomon was to build the Temple, and he did build it on the site chosen by his father. Mt. Moriah was already considered sacred by its earlier inhabitants, because the rock at the top was believed to be held in the mouth of the serpent Tahum, making that spot the intersection of the upper and lower worlds. The Hebrew people believed that it was the place where Abraham had been willing to sacrifice his son Isaac.

The construction of the Temple began around 950 and took seven years to complete. Solomon brought in craftsmen from Tyre, as well as wood from Lebanon's legendary cedar trees. The description of this construction is found in the Books of Kings in the Old Testament. This account tells us that the entire interior of the Temple—floors, ceilings, and walls—was covered in gold. That would take an estimated 45,000 pounds of gold. The work-force to complete this project was also enormous, with 80,000 stone quarries and 70,000 porters. The construction began with laying the foundation stone, something an organization in Israel has tried to do again in recent times.

The Temple contained a great basin called the Molten Sea. No one is sure what the purpose of this basin was, but its creation was amazing. It was cast in copper or bronze, weighed nearly thirty tons, and held about 10,000 gallons of water. There were also ten smaller basins used by the priest for ritual baths. The Sea may have been used in some rituals involving the sea or the primordial waters of Genesis.

The Temple was divided into two parts, the Temple proper and the Holy of Holies, where the Ark of the Covenant was kept. The Ark of the Covenant had been built under the direction of Moses during the time in the desert. It was a chest about $4 \times 2 \times 2$ feet, made of acacia wood overlaid with gold. It had four golden rings through which two poles of acacia overlaid with gold were passed in order to carry it during the time of wanderings. The cover was of gold and had two cherubim of solid gold facing each other with spread wings. No one knows exactly what a cherubim looked like, but many guess that they were winged, humanlike figures.

The Bible tells us that the Israelites were able to speak with God between the cherubim. It is also reported that there was a cloud over the Ark from which God spoke to them (Exod. 25:22; Lev. 16:2). When the Israelites were camped, the Ark was kept in the Tabernacle, a tent for that purpose. When the people moved on, the veil at the door of the Tabernacle was removed by the priests, then the Ark was wrapped in the veil before it was covered in animal skins and carried out, unseen by all but Moses and the priests.

In Solomon's Temple, the Holy of Holies was covered by veils of fine linen cloth dyed in the costly colors of hyacinth blue, purple, and scarlet. The Ark was against one wall and contained a golden vessel of manna, the food God had provided for the Israelites in the desert, and the rod of Aaron that had blossomed. The Tablets of the Law written by Moses, which many believe to be parts of Exodus and Leviticus, were either in the Ark or laid beside it in the Holy of Holies.

Jerusalem was besieged by the Babylonian king Nebuchadnezzar in 597 B.C.E. and the Temple treasures were taken away. Nebuchadnezzar's army came again in 586, ransacking Jerusalem, destroying Solomon' s Temple, and taking many people as captives. The Ark of the Covenant was never seen again. What happened to it? Some say that it was taken away by the Babylonians and destroyed after being stripped of its gold. Other accounts from a purported letter of Jeremiah and from the Jewish Talmud say that the Ark was hidden and will remain hidden until the Messiah comes. Another story says that the Ark was concealed for some time and is now in the possession of Christians in Africa.

Almost fifty years after Nebuchadnezzar's destruction of the first Temple, Babylon was defeated by Persia and the remnant of the Hebrew people returned to Jerusalem. Cyrus told them to rebuild the Temple, and they did this by 515.

In subsequent centuries, Jerusalem was conquered by several different empires. The Romans took control in 64 B.C.E. King Herod, who ruled (37–4 B.C.E.) under the Romans, was very fond of building, and he added to the Temple, including the addition of the Western Wall, which is now called the Wailing Wall. The second Temple was destroyed by the Roman army under Titus in 70 C.E., during a Hebrew rebellion against Rome, and the Hebrew people were scattered in what is called the Diaspora.

The Roman emperor Constantine and his mother, Empress Helena, converted to Christianity in the fourth century, and they built several Christian shrines in Jerusalem, including the Church of the Holy Sepulcher. Jerusalem remained a Christian city for 288 years until it was taken by Persians and then by Caliph Umar. Umar first built a mosque and then the Dome of the Rock on the mount.

The mount has special significance in Islam, because it is believed to be the place from which Mohammad ascended to Heaven to a vision of God. A golden ladder is said to have appeared on the mount, and Mohammad climbed it through seven heavens to receive instructions from Allah. On this journey, Mohammad met

Abraham, Moses, Jesus, and others, so this journey is seen as a continuation of the earlier traditions, not a creation of something new.

Construction of the Dome of the Rock continued from 687 to 691, and has stood in that place for 1,312 years. The two Jewish Temples stood on that spot for a total of 956 years. The Hebrew people of antiquity controlled the city for approximately 1,070 years, until the Diaspora. Modern Jews have controlled Jerusalem since the Six Day War in 1967 (the city was officially made the capital of Israel in 1980), for a total of 1,106 years, while Moslems have controlled the city for close to 1,200 years. It is easy to see why both of these groups claim the right to the city and why the removal of the Dome of the Rock would be such a serious matter.

Jerusalem was the site of many battles of the European Christian Crusades, and the Crusaders managed to control the city for approximately ninety years after 1099 C.E. During that time, the Church of the Holy Sepulcher, which had been destroyed, was rebuilt, and the Dome of the Rock was turned into a Christian shrine called *Templum Domini,* or "Temple of the Lord." Christians, who have controlled the city for less than 400 years, do not claim a right to control it now, but many important Christian shrines are located there.

JEWISH VIEWS ON THE TEMPLE

The traditional morning prayers said by all practicing Jewish males asks for the Temple in Jerusalem to be rebuilt. Since these prayers are a matter of long tradition, the different sects of Judaism agree on them. Agreement on practical realities is less universal.

One of the difficulties with a new Temple is the issue of animal sacrifice. The Temple in ancient times was primarily the site of sacrifices. Sin offerings were made there, sacrifices for ritual cleansing, and sacrifices as part of festivals. The Passover, for example, called for the slaughter of a lamb. The live lamb was purchased and taken to the Temple, where it was slaughtered. After the sacrifice, the meat was taken and consumed by the family. The scene of this slaughter would be horrifying to many modern sensibilities. The crowds, the screams of the animals, and the smell of the blood would all be overwhelming.

After the destruction of the second Temple and the Diaspora, the Hebrew people followed what is called rabbinic Judaism, which is a religion based on prayer and the study of scripture, rather than on the ritual sacrifices of live animals. The sacrifice of animals was a normal part of religion in antiquity, though Zarathrustra, the great Persian mystic, had tried to stop it. Today, very few religions practice animal sacrifice. One of the few that does so in the United States is the Santeria or Voodoo tradition from Africa. Court battles are being fought over local ordinances to protect animals from Santeria rituals. Since animals are regularly slaughtered for food, this may be a bit hypocritical for meat eaters, but it illustrates how much modern sensibilities recoil from the idea of watching an animal being killed, or of considering the killing of an animal to be an act of worship.

Many people within the Jewish community share these sensibilities. They do not want to return to a religion of animal sacrifice and resurrect the rituals of two thousand years ago. The difficulty is that if the Temple is rebuilt, the religious authorities are split on the consequences. Many believe that the Talmud requires that sacrifices resume if the Temple is rebuilt. This group includes people who do not want the sacrifices to resume. The most conservative

Orthodox Jews insist that sacrifices must be resumed and support the use of sacrifice. If a third Temple were built, therefore, it would be the cause of major disputes within Judaism, and might threaten the cohesiveness of the community in a way that two thousand years of diaspora did not.

EFFORTS TO REBUILD

In 1984, the Israeli government discovered that a Jewish terrorist group was planning to blow up the Dome of the Rock so that the Temple could be rebuilt. The conspiracy was discovered in time to be stopped. Since then, a group called the Temple Mount and Land of Israel Faithful Movement has been formed and is working openly to have the Temple rebuilt. In their literature, they refer to Moslems as "pagans," and insist that the Temple Mount must be returned to God, which for them means returned to Jewish control. They suggest that the Dome of the Rock be dismantled and moved to Mecca.[1]

This group claims that it knows God wants them to rebuild the Temple, since scripture shows that God wanted the Temple rebuilt in the past. They do not rely on any specific scripture to argue that past prophecies about the Temple have not been fulfilled, as we saw that a small group of Christians does. The Faithful Movement claims that real peace will come and all the problems of Israel will be resolved when the third Temple is built.

On October 20, 1997, this group brought a four-and-a-half-ton marble foundation stone to Jerusalem, with the intention of laying it on the Temple Mount. This event was held during the festival of the Feast of Tabernacles, when it is believed King Solomon first brought the Ark of the Covenant to the Temple Mount and into the first Temple. The group performed the same rites Solomon was said to have performed with the Ark and used the prayer and psalms of King David used by Solomon at his dedication of the first Hebrew altar on the Mount. The foundation stone was brought from a desert area of Israel, Mitzpe Ramon. It came from the land of a Jewish family named Alafi, which has a family tradition claiming that the family helped to build both of the Temples in Jerusalem. This family is reportedly preparing other stones for the third Temple.

When the foundation stone arrived in Jerusalem, the Israeli government refused to allow the group to put it on the Temple Mount, because it would have been a provocation to the Moslems who have their holy site there. The group satisfied itself by parading through Jerusalem, circling the old city area, and following various traditional rituals. The foundation stone is being kept for the day when the rebuilding of the Temple can begin.[2]

There is another preparation for the new Temple being made, and that relates to the Ceremony of the Red Heifer that is described in Numbers 19. That ceremony was a preliminary ceremony of the early Hebrews in order to make purification rites possible. Some believe that this ceremony must be carried out for the new Temple, the location of purification rites, to be built. The problem has been that it is difficult to find a pure red heifer without blemish. Clyde Lott, a Southern Baptist cattle breeder from Mississippi, decided to help, and he has bred cattle to produce a red heifer and shipped them to Israel. A red heifer was born in Israel on April 8, 2002, and has been declared kosher by rabbis. This is seen by some as a step toward rebuilding the Temple and a sign from God that he wants the Temple rebuilt. Lott is among the Christians who believe the Temple must be rebuilt before the Messiah will return.[3]

CHRISTIAN VIEW ON THE TEMPLE

The writings of first-century Christians show that they tended to believe that the destruction of Jerusalem and the second Temple was a judgment on the Jews because they handed over Jesus to the Romans and refused to accept him as the Jewish Messiah. That was definitely the view of the Church that evolved over the next few centuries. They believed that the Jews had forfeited their rights as the covenant people of God by their refusal to acknowledge God's Messiah, so it followed that the New Jerusalem and the new Temple would be heavenly or spiritual entities, not part of the material world. The New Jerusalem and Temple would be Christian, not Jewish. Many early Christians mentioned Jesus as the Temple of God. By sacrificing himself, they believed that Jesus had taken the place of any animal sacrifice. God himself had been sacrificed, and now no more sacrifice was needed. We see such a reference to the New Jerusalem in the Book of Revelation 21:10.

Modern Christians are a diverse group and have widely differing views on many things, including the End Time prophecies. The majority of Christians today agree that there is no need for the Temple in Jerusalem to be rebuilt before the Messiah returns. As we have seen, Dispensationalists and a few others believe that the Bible requires the Temple to be rebuilt before the End Time.

As we said in chapter 1, many modern scholars and theologians favor another interpretation of Daniel 9:24–27, the biblical text the Dispensationalists rely on for their conclusions. In approximately 169 B.C.E., Antiochus Epiphanes, leader of the Seleucid Empire, conquered Jerusalem. He agreed to a peace, but two years later he broke his word and pillaged the city, slaughtering many and taking ten thousand captives. He took all the Temple treasures, forbade many of the practices of the Jewish religion, destroyed sacred scrolls, and had a pagan altar set up in the Temple on which he had a pig sacrificed every day. Antiochus Epiphanes held the city for approximately three and a half years, until he was defeated in the Maccabean revolt. In 70 C.E., the Roman general and future emperor Titus sacked Rome, destroyed the Temple, and scattered the people.

Many commentators believe that the prophecy of Daniel was fulfilled in Antiochus Epiphanes, in one of the most accurate and detailed biblical fulfillments known. The prophecy of Jesus that the Temple would be destroyed was fulfilled by the destruction of the Temple in 70 C.E. Some argue that because it sounds like Jesus is saying that the destruction of the Temple and the End Time will come together, there has to be another Temple and another destruction before the prophecy will be fulfilled.

Others argue that the Temple was destroyed in 70 C.E., exactly as Jesus said it would be, and many believe that the End Time will also be as he described. As for when the End Time will come, we have to look to other prophecies.

THE RETURN OF ISRAEL

Though most Christians do not believe that the Temple has to be rebuilt before the Messiah can return, there is a strong feeling that the restoration of Israel is an important event leading up to the End Time. In the nineteenth century, there was a push to bring on the End Time before the turn of the twentieth century. William Hechler, chaplain at the British embassy in Germany, persuaded Kaiser Wilhelm II that a Jewish state was necessary for the fulfillment of prophecy. As a result, the Kaiser supported Zionism.[4]

This belief has also had a major impact on Western political relations with Israel. On May 14, 1948, then President Truman asked Special Council Clark Clifford to address the Cabinet in support of US recognition of a Jewish nation. In his address to the Cabinet, Clifford cited Deuteronomy for the argument that God had given the Palestinian strip to the Jews. We don't know which section he cited, but it may have been verse 30:5[5]: "And the LORD thy God will bring thee into the land which thy fathers possessed, and thou shalt possess it; and he will do thee good, and multiply thee above thy fathers."

Many biblical prophecies say that God will restore an Israel that has been scattered through all the nations. Many commentators, both Jewish and Christian, believe that this prophecy was not fulfilled in antiquity, because though a remnant of the Hebrew people was returned from Babylon, the scattered ten lost tribes did not return. The restoration of Israel in the twentieth century, on the other hand, saw Jews coming from all over the world to the land they considered their spiritual home. Now, many agree, the prophecy of the restoration of Israel has been fulfilled.

There is no prophecy linking the restoration of Israel to the building of a new Temple, something even the Israeli supporters of a new Temple admit. So there is no reason for a Temple to be built on the Temple Mount before the Messiah returns.

CHAPTER 11

THE END TIME

The End Time is the time after the Apocalypse or near the end of the apocalyptic period and just before the Messiah returns. It is also called the Latter Days in the Bible. The battle of Armageddon occurs during the End Time in the Book of Revelation. Some people assume that the End Time is really the end of the world as we know it and that the world of the Millennium will be populated by resurrected saints. Others think that the events of the Apocalypse will be so catastrophic that it will be the end of life or civilization as we know it.

As we have seen, the events of the twentieth century have been more catastrophic than any ancient prophet could have imagined. Images of bombing raids, the firebombing of Dresden and other cities, people gassed and buried in mass graves, whole areas, including the people in them, incinerated in atomic blasts, acid rain destroying whole forests, the depletion of the ozone layer letting in deadly radiation, the explosion of Chernobyl are enough to inspire the most extreme End Time prophecies. All this has already happened, and humanity may be ready for the spiritual renewal that will mark the coming of the Messiah. If so, the remainder of the End Time should be a time of transformation and renewal.

DO WE HAVE A CHOICE?

Biblical prophecy is supported by prophets from more modern times. Nostradamus prophesied about the End Time during the sixteenth century, and so did other more recent prophets like Edgar Cayce. All of these prophets were devout Christians who understood their prophecies to be consistent with the Bible.

Interpreters of Nostradamus have long been confused about his predictions for the end of the twentieth and the beginning of the twenty-first centuries. He seems to have predicted alternative scenarios for the same time period. On the one hand, he predicted a time of peace.

Pestilences extinguished, the world becomes smaller, for a long time the lands will be inhabited peacefully. People will travel safely through the sky, land, and sea: then wars will start up again (CI. V63).

Some commentators have suggested that this prediction refers to the twentieth century, but a rational look at the twentieth century and its series of wars, airplane hijackings, and terrorist threats tells us this prediction has not yet come to pass. The alternate predictions Nostradamus has made for this time foretell a time of major war and destruction that is to be followed by a time of peace:

The horrible war which is being prepared in the West, the following year will come the pestilence, so very horrible that young, old, nor beast [will survive]. Blood, fire Mercury, Mars, Jupiter in France (CIX. V55).

Mabus then will soon die. There will come of people and beasts a horrible rout: Then suddenly one will see vengeance, hundred, hand, thirst, hunger when the comet will run (CII. V62).

> *Mars and Jupiter under conjunction, a calamitous war*
> *under Cancer. A short time afterward a new king will be*
> *anointed who will bring peace to the earth for a long time*
> *(CVI. V24).*

If we assume that these predictions have not yet come true in the calamities of the twentieth century, then we appear to have an alternative prediction. Either we will have peace now, or we will have a terrible war and horrible calamities and then we will have peace. How will the choice be made?

Edgar Cayce gives us some insight into that. He, too, gave alternative predictions for this period of time. Cayce predicted many remarkable events for the end of the twentieth century that have not yet happened: much of the eastern and western coasts of the United States will be under water; major geological shifts; an inland sea in the United States linking the Great Lakes to the Gulf of Mexico; sudden changes in Europe; and some event that will make one think the earth has lost its natural gravitational movement and will be plunged into eternal darkness.[1]

Cayce, who was called the sleeping prophet because he gave readings in a trance state, said in some of his readings that the changes happening during this time period would be sudden and catastrophic. In other readings he said that the changes would be gradual and not catastrophic. When he was asked why there was a difference, he said:

> *[It] may depend upon much that deals with the metaphysical. . . .*
> *There are those conditions that in the activity of individuals,*
> *in line of thought and endeavor keep oft many a city and*
> *many a land intact through their application of spiritual laws.[2]*

In other words, both Nostradamus and Cayce tell us that the actions of humans in following spiritual laws affect the events of the world. This concept is supported by other, lesser-known prophecies. In 1917, three children in Fatima, Portugal, had a vision of Mary, the mother of Jesus. She warned them that the world would experience war unless the Catholic Church followed her advice. In the visions, she predicted the end of World War I, the rise of Russia as a world power, and mentioned a pope called Pius XI, who was elected in 1922. Mary's request in that vision was that the Church reach out to Russia by consecrating it to her immaculate heart. That would avert war and bring peace. The Church did not enact a consecration until 1984,[3] well into the Cold War, which was even more deadly than the larger conflict had been, with constant small wars fought around the world.[4] Could this have been averted if the request had been carried out in 1917?

Two unknown American women claim that they have also received messages from Mary. Veronica Lueken, a wife and mother of five, said that Mary has appeared to her for thirteen years at Rosary vigils in Flushing Meadow Park, Flushing, Queens. The message she received was very simple: The people of the world have a choice. They can choose spiritual renewal or they will experience a nuclear war and collision with a comet. In the process, many nations will disappear and three-fourths of mankind will die. Mary is quoted as saying: "The cure, if not given physically, I assure you, my children, will be given to you spiritually."

Another woman, in Georgia, Nancy Fowler, says she has been receiving messages from Mary since 1990, but expects to receive only one more. The message is essentially the same as the message to Lueken: "I come with a serious warning. A great war will come upon this world, greater than man has ever known. Pray, children, pray. Amend your ways, please."[5]

The war that we are warned about in both series of messages may be the same war Nostradamus describes in his alternative prediction. All of these prophets give us a similar message. The end of the twentieth century and the beginning of the twenty-first century is a time of great choice for humanity. Humanity has been repeatedly warned. It can choose spiritual renewal or a continuation of war. Since humanity has developed such horrible and destructive weapons, a major war will mean widespread devastation, but there is no reason for this to happen. Humanity now has the capacity to choose a time of peace.

Is this idea consistent with prophecy in the Bible? We've seen several rounds of beast-nations, Antichrist figures, and apocalyptic events, but the Messiah has not yet returned. Could that be connected?

One possibility is that Cayce and the other prophets are right. We have a choice about future events. The End Time will be catastrophic, but it may not be more catastrophic than it has already been. As this apocalyptic period ends, is it possible that the Messiah is about to return?

A SPIRITUAL RENEWAL

An answer to that question may be found in an interesting part of the Book of Revelation that is ignored by most commentators on End Time events. The Revelation begins with seven letters to seven churches, which are often dismissed as just historical letters to seven first-century congregations. We have seen that seven is a number of completion and of divine action. It is the most frequently used number in the Book of Revelation. The idea that these were just letters to historical churches does not stand up to closer scrutiny, as we will see in the next chapter. Every prophet and prophecy has a moral and spiritual message, and the Book of Revelation is no exception. To use it just as a map for future events is to disregard the most important aspect of the Revelation: what God's people need to hear, if they have the ears to listen.

There is another part of Revelation that is most likely connected to this message. John's vision portrays 144,000 people, 12,000 from each tribe of Israel, who will be sealed by God:

> *And after these things I saw four angels standing on the four corners of the earth, holding the four winds of the earth, that the wind should not blow on the earth, nor on the sea, nor on any tree. And I saw another angel ascending from the east, having the seal of the living God: and he cried with a loud voice to the four angels, to whom it was given to hurt the earth and the sea, saying, Hurt not the earth, neither the sea, nor the trees, till we have sealed the servants of our God in their foreheads. And I heard the number of them which were sealed: and there were sealed a hundred and forty and four thousand of all the tribes of the children of Israel (Rev. 7:1–4).*

The 144,000 are gathered by four angels from the four corners of the earth. They are mentioned in conjunction with a multitude that comes from every nation, every language group, every people. All of them are praising God; all of them are renewed. They are a multitude beyond count:

> *After this I beheld, and, lo, a great multitude, which no man could number, of all nations, and kindreds, and people, and tongues, stood before the throne, and before the Lamb, clothed with white robes, and palms in their hands; And cried with a*

loud voice, saying, Salvation to our God which sitteth upon the
throne, and unto the Lamb (Rev. 7:9–10).

Who are these people? We have seen that 144,000 is a number
of ultimate completion. This is a final resolution of the purpose of
the twelve, which for John includes the twelve tribes of Israel and the
twelve apostles of Jesus and of the Christian Church. Twelve times
twelve is 144, the number of perfect completion. The number 144
times 1,000 gives us the ultimate perfect completion: the resolution
of God's work on earth.

Since John was a Christian, it is not likely that he thought it was
literally only Jews who would be sealed by God. This is particularly
true since the twelve tribes of Israel had not been a reality for centuries. Ten of the original twelve tribes had been "lost" during battles with the Assyrians almost 600 years before. Jewish legend said
that they had been scattered into every nation of the world. This
explains the prophecies that the Jews would be gathered from the
nations. Since those ten tribes—the vast majority—were no longer
recognizable as Jews, and since John believed that God's people included Christians, it is likely that John is using the tribes of Israel
symbolically here. The twelve tribes of Israel represent the whole of
God's people on earth. At the end time they are from every nation,
every language group, every people. This is a description of inclusive unity, which John emphasizes repeatedly by talking about the
four corners of the earth, all the nations, and so on.

The 144,000 appear later in Revelation with Jesus on Mt. Zion,
and then an angel with a Gospel (good news) proclaims it to the
world:

And I saw another angel fly in the midst of heaven, having the
everlasting gospel to preach unto them that dwell on the earth,

and to every nation, and kindred, and tongue, and people,
saying with a loud voice, Fear God, and give glory to him; for
the hour of his judgement is come: and worship him that made
heaven, and earth, and the sea, and the fountains of waters
(Rev. 14:6–7).

Again, John emphasizes the universality of this message. All of this happens before the Messiah returns.

The theory that the story of the 144,000 and the multitude refers to a spiritual renewal is strengthened by the fact that these references in Revelation refer back to the Old Testament, particularly to the prophecy in Ezekiel that Israel will be spiritually renewed before the End Time and will no longer commit the same errors:

Neither will I cause men to hear in thee the shame of the hea-
then any more, neither shalt thou bear the reproach of the peo-
ple any more, neither shalt thou cause thy nations to fall any
more, saith the Lord GOD.

Moreover the word of the LORD came unto me, saying,
Son of man, when the house of Israel dwelt in their own
land, they defiled it by their own way and by their doings:
their way was before me as the uncleanness of a removed
woman (Ezek. 36:15–17).

There is also a prophecy in Jeremiah that God promises shepherds who will teach understanding so that all people can gather together in Jerusalem:

And I will give you pastors according to mine heart, which
shall feed you with knowledge and understanding. And it shall
come to pass, when ye be multiplied and increased in the land,
in those days, saith the LORD, they shall say no more, The ark

of the covenant of the LORD: neither shall it come to mind:
neither shall they remember it; neither shall they visit it; nei-
ther shall that be done any more. At that time they shall call
Jerusalem the throne of the LORD; and all the nations shall
be gathered unto it, to the name of the LORD, to Jerusalem:
neither shall they walk any more after the imagination of their
evil heart (Jer. 3:15–17).

Jeremiah became a prophet in the thirteenth year of the reign
of King Josiah, in 627 B.C.E. His work continued until Jerusalem
was conquered by Babylon around 587, though he continued some
work in Judah and Egypt after the fall of Jerusalem. The reign of
Josiah was marked by a religious nationalism and the belief that
Jerusalem, as the city of God with the Temple where God dwelt,
could not be conquered or destroyed (Pss. 46, 48).

It is fairly easy to imagine the outrage of the people when Jeremiah began to prophesy about God's judgment on Judah and to
predict the defeat of the nation. He was arrested and imprisoned
and subjected to a great deal of hostility for his predictions, which
turned out to be only too correct. Jeremiah dictated a scroll and sent
it to king Jehoiakim, who threw it into the fire. Jehoiakim was the
king who provoked the Babylonian invasion of Judah that fulfilled
Jeremiah's worst predictions.

The Book of Jeremiah is the longest book of the Old Testament
in the original Hebrew writing. In it Jeremiah describes the failure
of the nation in its worship of God and the punishment God will
inflict. He also writes what is called the book of consolation, showing there is still hope beyond national disaster. Jeremiah claimed
that a prophet who does not challenge the conscience of the nation
is not a true prophet (Jer. 23:9–40).

There is good reason to believe that the return of the Messiah will be marked not just by the threat of a beast-nation and Antichrist, apocalyptic events, or great battle, but that it will also be marked by a spiritual renewal that will sweep the world and will unite people from all races, nations, and religions.

CHOOSING MORE APOCALYPSE

But what if we do not choose a spiritual renewal? What do the prophets suggest will happen then? We have already seen that there are two major predictions that are also consistent with the Book of Revelation. These predictions are that we will have a major and devastating nuclear war and that the earth will collide with a meteorite.

We have probably all heard of or thought of scenarios for a nuclear war. First comes the nuclear blast that kills the lucky ones instantly, and then comes the nuclear winter, where deadly radiation sickness spreads throughout the planet. Most of us have heard reports of the horrors of the atomic bombs dropped on Japan at the end of World War II.

Modern one-megaton bombs are fifty times the size of the bombs dropped on Japan. These larger bombs do not destroy a much larger area, but they release more deadly radiation. Dropped on any major city, such as London, New York, Munich, Moscow, or Tokyo, a one-megaton bomb would probably kill up to a million people, depending on the time of day or night and the fluctuation of populations in the city centers. In addition, there would be up to a million and a half injured around the edges of the circle. To completely destroy a megacity like London, New York, or Moscow would take several megaton weapons—three or four would do it.

According to prophecies in the Book of Revelation, we will face an overshadowing of the sun, moon, and stars, and much of the day will have no light during the final apocalypse. This is a classic symptom of the presence of volcanic dust in the atmosphere that blocks out light, such as has happened during the biggest volcanic eruptions in our history—for example, Krakatoa, which erupted in 1883. But there is unlikely to be a volcanic eruption big enough to block out a third of the earth's exposure to the sun. A more likely scenario is the arrival of a massive meteorite that crashes into the earth and sends up masses of dust into the atmosphere. This is consistent with the predictions of modern prophets.

Scientists have recently discovered more evidence of past collisions with meteorites. One that occurred almost 3.5 billion years ago left debris in South Africa and Australia. Evidence collected indicates that this meteorite was only twelve miles across. A meteorite half that size, six miles across, is believed to have caused such a radical shift in the earth's climate that it resulted in the extinction of the dinosaurs about sixty-five million years ago.

When a meteorite collides with the earth, it passes through the atmosphere in about one second, leaving a hole or vacuum behind. Before the air in the atmosphere can move in to fill that hole, the meteorite hits and melts and vaporizes rock, sending that vapor directly into the atmosphere. This cloud spreads around the earth. Eventually, the cloud will condense and solid bits of rock will rain back on the earth, which could be the hail of Revelation. The collision sixty-five million years ago left "rained" rock deposits only two centimeters deep, but the collision 3.5 billion years ago left deposits twenty to thirty centimeters thick, which could cause widespread damage to plants and agriculture. Acid rain, caused by vaporized sulfur that becomes sulfuric acid, would follow. The dust cloud would last long enough to cause the climate to cool, and this cooling is what is believed to have caused the extinction of the dinosaurs.

That scenario occurs if a meteorite hits dry land. If it hits an ocean, there are more disastrous results. The impact would generate enormous, miles-high tsunamis in seconds, devastating and eroding away coastal areas and damaging the ocean floor. The impact of an asteroid can also cause an axis shift of the earth, causing major climate shifts.

In 1994, Comet Shoemaker-Levy 9 broke into twenty pieces and hit Jupiter. The impact of several of the pieces caused fireballs as large as the earth. In 1998, Brian Marsden, astronomer for the Harvard-Smithsonian Center for Astrophysics, predicted that a mile-wide asteroid (Asteroid 1997XF11) could hit earth in the year 2028 or pass within 30,000 miles. Scientists have since calculated that it will miss the earth by 600,000 miles. But a slight bump from another asteroid could put it directly on a course for earth.[6]

If we choose spiritual renewal over war and collision with an asteroid, what does that mean? To find that out, we have to take a closer look at the letters that begin the Book of Revelation.

CHAPTER 12

SPIRITUAL RENEWAL

A UNIVERSAL MESSAGE

The Book of Revelation begins with seven letters written to the churches in the cities of Ephesus, Smyrna, Pergamum, Thyatira, Sardis, Philadelphia, and Laodicea. Almost all interpretations have taken these at little more than their face value— as letters to the churches of the time, written by John, instructing them how to behave in a time of religious persecution—but we will see that they contain a more universal message and a guide to spiritual renewal.

The seven cities in Revelation probably were not chosen simply for their religious or geographic significance. The word "city" was used in a different sense in those times. It meant something similar to a county and referred to the whole district in which the urban center was located. The province of Asia contained some one hundred and fifty cities altogether, and these seven cities happen to be located close to where Revelation was said to have been written, on the island of Patmos.

Pergamum, Ephesus, and Smyrna were certainly the most important three cities in the province, from the point of view of their influence and size, and it is quite possible that Sardis and Laodicea ranked fourth and fifth in size and importance. But the remaining two cities cannot have been included because of their size. Cyzicus was certainly a more important place than either Philadelphia or Thyatira, and we know, from an inscription on a coin of the Roman Emperor Gordian III, that the seventh-most-important city was Magnesia. So size was not the determining factor for the selection of these cities.

Nor can the list be a matter of the precedence of the Christian churches, because the church at Colossae, near Laodicea, was older and more important than those of the chosen cities, going back a generation to the days of Paul.

So the purpose of these letters probably was not related to the importance or size of the cities that they addressed, and in fact, placing them within the context of the rest of Revelation, there might not seem to be any reason for having the letters at all unless they contain some deeper significance. A close examination will show that each of these seven cities was connected to astrological signs and mythical figures, which can help us to understand their meaning.

Theology professor Ramsey Michaels writes:

Quite possibly John's choice of seven out of all the congregations that existed in Asia Minor at the time he wrote was a literary device related to his symbolic use of the number seven through-out his book. . . . The Muratorian Canon, probably in the late 2nd century, argued that John chose to write to seven churches as a way of addressing the whole church throughout the world, and found in this a parallel with the seven churches to which Paul wrote letters.[1]

To find John's universal message to the world, let us examine the texts of the letters.

LETTER TO EPHESUS

Unto the angel of the church of Ephesus write; These things saith he that holdeth the seven stars in his right hand, who walketh in the midst of the seven golden candlesticks;

I know thy works, and thy labour, and thy patience, and how thou canst not bear them which are evil: and thou hast tried them which say they are apostles, and are not, and hast found them liars: And hast borne, and hast patience, and for my name's sake hast laboured, and hast not fainted. Nevertheless I have somewhat against thee, because thou hast left thy first love. Remember therefore from whence thou art fallen, and repent, and do the first works; or else I will come unto thee quickly, and will remove thy candlestick out of his place, except thou repent. But this thou hast, that thou hatest the deeds of the Nicolaitanes, which I also hate. He that hath an ear, let him hear what the Spirit saith unto the churches; To him that overcometh will I give to eat of the tree of life, which is in the midst of the paradise of God (Rev. 2:1–7).

The predominant symbolism in this verse is derived from the connections of Ephesus with the goddess Artemis, whose presence dominated the city. The temple of Artemis located there was regarded as one of the seven wonders of the world of the time. Artemis represented the Great Mother and her astrological sign was Cancer, which is ruled astrologically by the Moon.

The symbol of Artemis was the bee, and the image of a bee appeared on coins as a symbol of Ephesus. The bee is the symbol of the Great Goddess in Asiatic traditions. Greek thought also associated Artemis with the Virgin Queen. A statue of Artemis in Ephesus shows her with many breasts, or what some commentators have described as the ova of the sacred bee. Bees are shown on the statue. There was also a legend that Mary died and was buried in Ephesus.[2]

As a great mother, Artemis is loving, diligent, and productive. In this letter, the congregation at Ephesus is congratulated for its ability to discriminate between good and evil, between falsity and truth. However, it is criticized for abandoning its first love. The ancient Hebrew teaching (Lev. 19:18) about loving others as you love yourself was repeated by Jesus several times (Matt. 19:19, 22:39; Mark 12:31; Luke 10:27). This means that spiritual love begins with the love of oneself as the image of God, the love of what is Godlike in the self. Then others are loved in that same way: for their nature as the image of God. In its discrimination between good and evil, truth and falsity, the congregation at Ephesus has forgotten the most important thing: love. A wise person discriminates in love. An unwise person forgets about love and becomes judgmental.

The first message for the spiritual renewal is to remember that love is the most important thing. Like the unconditional love of the great mother, our love nurtures and supports life. All understanding and all action must begin with and arise out of love.

LETTER TO SMYRNA

And unto the angel of the church in Smyrna write; These things saith the first and the last, which was dead, and is alive;

I know thy works, and tribulation, and poverty, (but thou art rich) and I know the blasphemy of them which say they are Jews, and are not, but are the synagogue of Satan. Fear none of those things which thou shalt suffer: behold, the devil shall cast some of you into prison, that ye may be tried; and ye shall

have tribulation ten days: be thou faithful unto death, and I
will give thee a crown of life. He that hath an ear, let him hear
what the Spirit saith unto the churches; He that overcometh
shall not be hurt of the second death (Rev. 2:8–11).

The city of Smyrna dates back to more than a thousand years
before Christ, when it was founded as an Aeolian Greek colony
that was then captured by Ionian Greeks. Around 600 B.C.E., it
was destroyed by the Lydians and then rebuilt from a design given
by Alexander the Great to the Macedonian general Lysimachus.
This design came from a dream that Alexander had in which the
goddess of Smyrna, Nemesis, gave the full plan of the new city
to him.

The goddess Nemesis, who appeared in a double form as the
figures Fate and Fortune, seems to associate most closely with the
astrological characteristics of the Virgo-Pisces polarity—Virgo being
the process that is born out of the death of one life and the birth of
another when Capricornian ambition and rationality have turned
toward self-discovery. Virgo also epitomizes the physical conditions
of life—that is, the body, health, and work to sustain the body.
Pisces is further associated with the unconscious. Once the individual, for example, abandons work that is done simply for financial gain, there might be an opportunity to find new pastures
through greater self-reflection.

The message to the congregation at Smyrna is consistent with
this symbolism. The congregation is rich, but its real condition is
poverty. The New Revised Standard Version translates Revelation
2:9 as "I know your affliction and your poverty, even though you
are rich." The ambition of the congregation has been worldly and
material. Because it has material comfort, it thinks it is rich. These
people have not yet realized that real riches are the riches of the

spirit and the riches of the heart. A person with great material wealth and little self-awareness is a pauper. A person with self-awareness, with spiritual understanding, is rich no matter how much material wealth he or she has. It is not necessary to be materially poor in order to be rich in spirit, but it is essential to be rich in spirit to avoid being poor.

LETTER TO PERGAMUM

And to the angel of the church in Pergamos write; These things saith he which hath the sharp sword with two edges;

I know thy works, and where thou dwellest, even where Satan's seat is: and thou holdest fast my name, and hast not denied my faith, even in those days wherein Antipas was my faithful martyr, who was slain among you, where Satan dwelleth. But I have a few things against thee, because thou hast there them that hold the doctrine of Balaam, who taught Balak to cast a stumbling block before the children of Israel, to eat things sacrificed unto idols, and to commit fornication. So hast thou also them that hold the doctrine of the Nicolaitans, which thing I hate. Repent; or else I will come unto thee quickly, and will fight against them with the sword of my mouth. He that hath an ear, let him hear what the Spirit saith unto the churches; To him that overcometh will I give to eat of the hidden manna, and will give him a white stone, and in the stone a new name written, which no man knoweth saving he that receiveth it (Rev. 2:12–17).

Pergamum was known for its interest in education, reasoning, and religious faith, thus giving us the polarity of Gemini and Sagittarius. The presiding deity at Pergamum was Athene, who was venerated as goddess of the arts and prudent intelligence.

The letter refers to the biblical story of Balaam and Balak. In this parable a diviner named Balaam was called upon by Balak, King of Moab, to put a curse on the Children of Israel while they remained camped in the land of Moab on their way to the Promised Land. Balak wished to get rid of these people and expected Balaam to use his considerable psychic powers to help him. God intervened and used Balaam for an oracle to Balak instead (Num. 22–24). In this letter, Balaam is still seen as the agent of the pagan opposition to God's will. Pergamum was also the home of Aesclepius, the god who had powers of healing. We still use the symbol of the serpent-entwined staff of Aesclepius. Originally the mythological staff of Hermes, it is now known as the Caduceus: the modern symbol of the healing arts.[3]

The congregation at Pergamum is criticized for fornication. As we saw in chapter 5, fornication in the Old Testament often refers to the worship of pagan gods, as it clearly does here. The people are eating the meat that has been sacrificed by the pagans. At that time, meat would be offered to the pagan gods and then eaten by the community after the offering. Since eating this meat is mentioned so often in the New Testament, it seems that many Christians saw no harm in it. The issue, however, is much larger than the question of eating the meat. The people who did this were not being true to their beliefs. They were making compromises, which probably made their life in the wider community easier. They were not being false in the sense that they were worshiping the pagan gods, but they were compromising for convenience. They were not being true to themselves, without regard for what others thought. They were making intellectual rationalizations.

If they are true to what they know without compromise, they are promised a form of spiritual initiation. They will move to a new level of understanding that is symbolized by the receipt of a white stone from Jesus, which contains a new and secret name. The giving of a new name was a symbol of spiritual initiation. We still see it today—for example, in the Catholic sacrament of confirmation, where the person being confirmed chooses a new name.

LETTER TO THYATIRA

And unto the angel of the church in Thyatira write; These things saith the Son of God, who hath his eyes like unto a flame of fire, and his feet are like fine brass;

I know thy works, and charity, and service, and faith, and thy patience, and thy works; and the last to be more than the first. Notwithstanding I have a few things against thee, because thou sufferest that woman Jezebel, which calleth herself a prophetess, to teach and to seduce my servants to commit fornication, and to eat things sacrificed unto idols. And I gave her space to repent of her fornication; and she repented not. Behold, I will cast her into a bed, and them that commit adultery with her into great tribulation, except they repent of their deeds. And I will kill her children with death; and all the churches shall know that I am he which searcheth the reins and hearts: and I will give unto every one of you according to your works. But unto you I say, and unto the rest in Thyatira, as many as have not this doctrine, and which have not known the depths of Satan, as they speak; I will put upon you none other burden. But that which ye have already hold fast till I come. And he that overcometh, and keepeth my works unto the end, to him will I give power over the nations:

And he shall rule them with a rod of iron; as the vessels of a potter shall they be broken to shivers: even as I received of my Father. And I will give him the morning star. He that hath an ear, let him hear what the Spirit saith unto the churches (Rev. 2:18–29).

The pagan deities most actively worshipped in the city of Thyatira at that time were the divine smith Hephaestus and the goddess Pallas Athene—Mars and Venus being their ruling planets, with the astrological signs Aries (Mars) and Libra (Venus) as polar and gender opposites.

The author uses another story from the Old Testament here, the infamous Jezebel, Phoenician Queen of Ahab, King of Israel (1 Kings 18–19, 21). In the twentieth century she has become a byword for sinful behavior, but, as in the letter to Pergamum, the theme is about luring people away from the truth, just as Jezebel wanted to convert her Hebrew husband to paganism. Her sin was not sexual but theological. The congregation in Thyatira is criticized for tolerating someone who is leading people astray.

In the same way that the symbolism connected to the city is about the balance of the male and female, the masculine and feminine, this warning is about balance. We saw in the letter to Ephesus that it is important to begin with love and to discriminate between good and bad, truth and falsity. Being loving does not mean that "anything goes." The congregation needs to stand up for truth, whatever the cost, and not be tolerant of evil in their midst. They have been warned to do this in a loving and nonjudgmental way. The trick is to learn this balance, to learn how to create a harmony of love, nonjudgment, and truth so that lies are not allowed to disturb the harmony of the community.

LETTER TO SARDIS

And unto the angel of the church in Sardis write; These things saith he that hath the seven Spirits of God, and the seven stars;

I know thy works, that thou hast a name that thou livest, and art dead. Be watchful, and strengthen the things which remain, that are ready to die: for I have not found thy works per-

fect before God. Remember therefore how thou hast received and heard, and hold fast, and repent. If therefore thou shalt not watch, I will come on thee as a thief, and thou shalt not know what hour I will come upon thee. Thou hast a few names even in Sardis which have not defiled their garments; and they shall walk with me in white: for they are worthy. He that overcometh, the same shall be clothed in white raiment; and I will not blot out his name out of the book of life, but I will confess his name before my Father, and before his angels. He that hath an ear, let him hear what the Spirit saith unto the churches (Rev. 3:1–6).

Sardis, of all the cities used in John's allegory of spiritual evolution, is the one most closely associated with ruling power. The city lay northeast of Ephesus on a spur of Mount Timolus, and its history went back some one thousand years before Christ. It was taken by Alexander in 334 B.C.E., and then became an administrative center under the Seleucid dynasty, which subsequently comprised the capital of a Roman federation. The goddess adopted by Sardis was Cybele, who was represented by two lions, giving us the astrological connection with Leo.

The characteristics of Leo are courage, dominance, and self-expression, providing us with our first hints of the intended allegory. The sign that lies opposite Leo on the zodiac is Aquarius, and we can make this link with Sardis from the inscription used on the coins in Sardis at the time—"Sardis, the First Metropolis of Asia, and of Lydia and of Hellenism." The main characteristics of Aquarius are a search for freedom within a social environment.

The message to the congregation at Sardis is "you are dead." These are people who have fallen asleep. They aren't paying attention to what is important. They may have become caught up in making a living, raising a family, and seeking after power, but they have forgotten to be ready for the return of the Messiah. This is the letter in which the necessity of a spiritual renewal is most clear. Wake up! The Messiah will come in the night when you are least expecting it. This is a common theme in the teachings of Jesus: Always be ready, because you never know when I will come (Mark 13:32–37; Matt. 24:42–51, 25:1–13; Luke 12:37–40). Revelation 16:15 says, "Behold, I come as a thief. Blessed is the one who stays awake and keeps his garments." A similar warning is found in the early Christian manual the Didache:

> *Watch over your life: let your lamps be not quenched and your loins be not ungirded, but be ready, for ye know not the hour in which our Lord cometh. 2. But be frequently gathered together seeking the things which are profitable for your souls, for the whole time of your faith shall not profit you except ye be found perfect at the last time.[4]*

The spiritual person is always conscious, always aware, always ready. The lamp is full to light the way if the bridegroom comes. This is what Buddhists call mindfulness, paying attention at all times. This is a warning to be prepared for the Messiah and expect him when you would least expect him, in this very moment.

LETTER TO PHILADELPHIA

And to the angel of the church in Philadelphia write; These things saith he that is holy, he that is true, he that hath the key of David, he that openeth, and no man shutteth; and shutteth, and no man openeth;

I know thy works: behold, I have set before thee an open door, and no man can shut it: for thou hast a little strength, and hast kept my word, and hast not denied my name. Behold, I will make them of the synagogue of Satan, which say they are Jews, and are not, but do lie; behold, I will make them to come and worship before thy feet, and to know that I have loved thee. Because thou hast kept the word of my patience, I also will keep thee from the hour of temptation, which shall come upon all the world, to try them that dwell upon the earth. Behold, I come quickly: hold that fast which thou hast, that no man take thy crown. Him that overcometh will I make a pillar in the temple of my God, and he shall go no more out: and I will write upon him the name of my God, and the name of the city of my God, which is new Jerusalem, which cometh down out of heaven from my God: and I will write upon him my new name. He that hath an ear, let him hear what the Spirit saith unto the churches (Rev. 3:7–13).

Ancient Philadelphia was located about a hundred miles due east of Smyrna and twenty-six miles southwest of Sardis on the Cogamis River, a tributary of the Hermus. It was established in 189 B.C.E., and so it was a relatively young city compared to many others in Turkey. The city guarded an important pass through the mountains between the Hermus and Meander river valleys. It stood on two important roads, one leading from Smyrna to the East, another coming from Rome via Pergamum and Sardis. All east-west trade passed through Philadelphia.

The city's founder was King Eumenes II of Pergamum (197–160 B.C.E.), who named it for his brother and successor, Attalus II (159–138). The trustworthiness and loyalty of Attalus had earned him the nickname Philadelphos (one who loves his brother). Eumanes established Philadelphia as a missionary city to spread the language and customs of Greece throughout the eastern parts of

Lydia and Phrygia. His intent was to promote a unity of spirit and loyalty throughout his realm. The city came under the jurisdiction of Rome (in 133 B.C.E.).

In 17 C.E. a great earthquake destroyed Philadelphia and eleven other cities in the area. While Sardis to the northwest seems to have suffered the most, Philadelphia experienced dangerous tremors for the next twenty years, keeping the citizens in a state of fear. Because of the constant fear of aftershocks, most of the people lived in huts outside the city and worked the fertile soil in the countryside.

For centuries after the time of John and Paul, Philadelphia remained a Christian city, even after the Turks and Islam spread across Asia Minor. It was not until the mid–fourteenth century that it came under Islamic control. Today the Turkish town of Alasehir occupies the site, but a Christian presence remains.

From the very beginning Philadelphia was seen as a monument to the possibility of divinity within mankind. The early-twentieth-century Russian mystic G. I. Gurdjieff emphasized the importance of this message by saying that everyone must find the way to Philadelphia, to brotherly love. The congregation in Philadelphia is the only one that isn't criticized in the Book of Revelation. They have been patient, enduring, and loving. Brotherly love is the essential key, to see and relate to the image of God in each other. This is something that may not be rewarded in a world that is out of balance with greed and lust for power, but, whatever the costs, the rewards will be well worth the effort.

LETTER TO LAODICEA

And unto the angel of the church of the Laodiceans write;
These things saith the Amen, the faithful and true witness, the
beginning of the creation of God;
I know thy works, that thou art neither cold nor hot: I

would thou wert cold or hot. So then because thou art luke-warm, and neither cold nor hot, I will spue thee out of my mouth. Because thou sayest, I am rich, and increased with goods, and have need of nothing; and knowest not that thou art wretched, and miserable, and poor, and blind, and naked: I counsel thee to buy of me gold tried in the fire, that thou mayest be rich; and white raiment, that thou mayest be clothed, and that the shame of thy nakedness do not appear; and anoint thine eyes with eyesalve, that thou mayest see. As many as I love, I rebuke and chasten: be zealous therefore, and repent. Behold, I stand at the door, and knock: if any man hear my voice, and open the door, I will come in to him, and will sup with him, and he with me. To him that overcometh will I grant to sit with me in my throne, even as I also overcame, and am set down with my Father in his throne.

He that hath an ear, let him hear what the Spirit saith unto the churches (Rev. 3:14–22).

Laodicea was founded by Antiochus II, grandson of Seleucus I, founder of the Seleucid dynasty. Antiochus named the city after his wife, Laodice. The city was well known for its commerce and became the banking and financial exchange center for the Roman emperors. The sign of Taurus best represents these characteristics—the psychological impulse to accumulate. Taurus is seen as the sign that rules virility and increase. Its opposite on the zodiac is Scorpio, which in turn balances the city's characteristics with resourcefulness and rejuvenation—the seed to bring still more wealth and success.

The deity most closely associated with the city is Zeus, the supreme god of the Greeks, protector of laws and morality. This wise sovereign gives us a symbol of leadership.

Power and money are seen for what they really are—not something to be accumulated as ends in themselves but merely as the outer representations of inner creativity. Money is the material expression of psychological energy. We have the energy and the life, and therefore we can simply use money as a device to help us create.

The congregation at Laodicea, however, had not learned this lesson. They have no passion in their life. They are neither hot nor cold. They are clearly not in touch with God, because it is not possible to be in touch with God without being passionate. These people think material prosperity is enough. They settle for comfort instead of the joy of spiritual experience. As a result, they are really miserable, and so unconscious that they don't even realize it. Real riches come from going through the fire of spiritual renewal, of having the dross burned away, leaving pure gold. This is the only gold with real value. Those who conquer are those who are purified in this way.

These letters repeatedly say that this message is for those who have the ears to listen. In other words, it is for people who have reached a sufficient level of spiritual development to understand the message and take it to heart.

CHAPTER 13

THE MESSIAH

Many people in all three of the religious traditions including and arising out of Judaism—Judaism, Christianity, and Islam—are expecting some kind of Messiah to appear after a time of difficulty and to bring in a period of peace in which the forces of good prevail over the forces of evil. The concepts of the nature and characteristics of this Messiah are not all the same.

THE JEWISH MESSIAH

There are many references to messianic figures in the Old Testament, and there was no one single idea about the Messiah in ancient Judaism. The word *messiah* in Hebrew means "anointed one." The word was used thirty times in the Hebrew Bible to refer to kings. It can also mean an anointed high priest.[1] There has been much diversity in Judaism throughout its history, and so there were many different expectations about who or what the Messiah would be. In spite of that, there was significant agreement that some kind of Messiah would come. Thus, it is not surprising that when some Jews in the first century claimed Jesus was the Messiah, many others didn't believe them, because he didn't fit their idea of the Messiah. Also, there were several men claiming to be the Messiah at that time, some of them leading people in resistance battles against Rome that led to many deaths and did not produce any Jewish victory. Understandably, some people were uneasy about claims to messiahship.

There were two general concepts about the Messiah in the Old Testament. One was that he would be what is called a reigning Messiah—that is, he would be an actual ruler, a king here on earth. This idea was connected to the belief that the royal house of King David, which had died out in Megiddo, would be brought back by God, because the rule of that line was a divinely ordained kingship. In support of that idea of the Messiah we find language like "authority, glory and power" (Dan. 7:13–14); "the everlasting kingdom" (Dan. 2:44–45); "the righteous branch" (Jer. 23:5–6); "the branch" (Zech. 6:12, 13); and "the ruler" (Mic. 5:2). This idea of the Messiah is called restorative messianism, or an expectation that something from the past, the Golden Age, will be restored.

There was also a different image of the Messiah in early Judaism, and that was the image of the suffering Messiah. This Messiah would be killed as a criminal but would really bear the sins of many (Isa. 53:12); he would be rejected and despised (Isa. 53:3, Ps. 69:4); and his friends would betray him (Ps. 41:9).

The Jewish Messiah was seen as a human being, not God. He was specially chosen by God as early as the time of Creation, and, as the suffering Messiah, he willingly agreed to suffer to save humanity, or the Jewish people, but he was not God. He would be born as a human being on the earth and would live and die in a normal way. Still, his coming would usher in the return of the divine kingdom on earth, so he was connected to supernatural events.

The Dead Sea Scroll manuscripts were found in the 1940s.

They date from between 200 B.C.E. and 70 C.E., with most of them earlier. These documents indicate that the Qumran community was expecting three Messiahs: a prophet, a priest, and a king.[2]

During the second century, when Christianity was growing as an independent religion, rabbinic Judaism explained the conflict between the two expectations for a Messiah by continuing the belief in multiple Messiahs. Some of the rabbis said that there would be two Messiahs: Messiah ben David and Messiah ben Joseph, and that is why the descriptions of the Messiahs are so different. Messiah ben Joseph would be the warrior that many Jewish people expected. He would fight and defeat Gog and Magog, and then he would be killed in battle (Ps. 22). After Messiah ben Joseph's death, Messiah ben David would become the sole king of the earth.

In this interpretation, Messiah ben Joseph is the expected suffering Messiah. He will fight and die, giving up his life to defeat the forces of evil. The connection between the suffering servant prophesied in Isaiah and Messiah ben Joseph was made clear in the *Aggada,* a legend from the Talmud. Messiah ben David is the expected reigning Messiah. He will rule the whole earth in accordance with God's will and the forces of good in a kingdom that will never end.

The return of the Messiah is a basic tenet of Judaism, though many people today do not think about it or discuss it very much. For those who believe that the Messiah is going to return after a time of great trial and after the battle to defeat Israel's enemies and the forces of evil, they may not be clear on what they expect. They may expect a warrior leader, a person who uses military force to protect Israel. (This might account for some of the political support for hard-line leaders in Israel.) Or they may expect someone who dies defending Israel. The one thing that is fairly clear is that they would be likely to expect a Jewish Messiah, someone who will defend and promote Judaism as against the other world religions, including

Christianity. They may believe that the other religions, like Christianity and Islam, will recognize that the real Messiah had not come before and that Judaism is still the covenant religion; it has not been replaced by Christianity or by Islam.

THE CHRISTIAN MESSIAH

There is no question that the picture of the Christian Messiah is the clearest in any of these three traditions. Christians uniformly expect Jesus to return as the Messiah. Christians believe that he has already come once as the Messiah. At that time, he came in the form of the suffering Messiah of Isaiah and the Psalms. He was hated and condemned. He suffered and died as a criminal, and he did this to take on himself the sins of humanity, so that humanity could be saved. Christians basically unanimously agree that this was a fulfillment of Jewish scripture and the coming of the Messiah that was expected by many in the first century.

Early Christian writers went to a lot of trouble to document the story of Jesus' life to show how he had fulfilled the ancient prophecies. At the time of early Christianity, there was a lot of debate about the accuracy of these claims. Jewish dissenters, for example, claimed that Jesus was born in Nazareth, not Bethlehem, so he did not fulfill that prophecy. Modern scholars in the Age of Aquarius are picking up that discussion where the ancients left off and questioning whether the New Testament accounts are literally true, or if they were created for the purpose of proving Jesus was the Messiah whose coming had been foretold. Despite that Aquarian-style questioning, the faith of millions of Christians remains unshaken. They are convinced that Jesus is the Messiah predicted by the Old Testament prophets.

When it comes to the question of the return of Jesus, we find a bit more disagreement. Some Christians argue that Jesus fulfilled all the prophecies when he lived on earth. He was the expected suffering Messiah, and he suffered and died for the sins of the world. They say he was also the reigning Messiah, because he ushered in the Kingdom of God. The Kingdom of God is a spiritual kingdom that will last forever, and which Jesus, in his divine form, will rule forever. They expect Jesus to be present in some form at the last Judgment or when each person is judged at death, but they do not expect him to be a reigning Messiah on earth.

Other Christians believe that the prophecies of the Old Testament will be literally fulfilled and that the prophecy of the Book of Revelation is correct. Jesus will actually return in some way and will either rule the earth or will resurrect saints from the dead who will rule the earth in his stead. His arrival will either begin or will herald the beginning of the Millennium, or one thousand years of peace and prosperity.

These Christians expect Jesus to be a Christian Messiah and to defend and protect Christianity. They expect Jews to realize that they were mistaken when they rejected Jesus as the person who fulfilled their messianic prophecies. When Jesus returns, it will be obvious that he was the Messiah all along, and the Jewish people will repent and will convert to Christianity. People from other religious traditions will also realize that Jesus is the Messiah and the Son of God and will convert to Christianity.

THE ISLAMIC MESSIAH

The Islamic tradition of messianic figures is not based on actual text of the Qur'an but on *hadith,* or traditions about the saying of Mohammad, the Prophet of Islam. The *hadith* are not part of the text of the Qur'an, which was dictated by an angelic messenger. Because the different sects of Islam have different records of *hadith*, they don't all agree on what to expect.

One belief, most common among Shii,[3] is that *al-Mahdi*, "the rightly guided one," will come to usher in an era of justice and true belief before the final end of the world. The title "Mahdi" was originally used as an honorific title for prominent men in Islam. It was used, for example, as a title for the Prophet, the first four caliphs (rulers of Islam), and for Muhammad ibn al-Hanafiya, the son of Ali, the son-in-law of the prophet and fourth caliph. It later came to mean an expected ruler who would restore the glory of Islam.

Some believe that the Mahdi has already come one time. They believe he was the son of the twelfth imam, who died in 874 C.E. The child, Muhammad, was said to be five or six years old at the time of his father's death, and many expected him to succeed his father and become the thirteenth imam. But instead, people believed that the child went into concealment or occultation soon after his father's death. He will return at the end time. His concealment had two stages, the lesser concealment, which ended in approximately 939 C.E., and the greater concealment, which will not end until the end of time, when he returns. This idea is based on the belief that God would not leave the world without an imam, so the imam must be hidden but still in the world.

The Mahdi is expected to appear when the world has reached its worst state, but to bring in a time of abundance, justice, and faith, and defeat the enemies of Islam. He will be generous and will divide the wealth of the world in a fair way.

The return of the Mahdi is also often associated with the return of Jesus, though it should be pointed out that there is no idea in Islam that either the Mahdi or Jesus is God. The Qur'an is emphatic that the idea that Jesus is actually God is mistaken (Q. 4:171–73; 5:17, 116–118; 6:100–03; etc.). Nevertheless, the Qur'an teaches that Jesus, who is called *al-haqq*, "the word of truth," was born in a virgin birth by the will of God (Q. 3:42). Jesus is considered to be one of the great prophets of Islam and the earlier traditions of Judaism and Christianity (Q. 3:48–63, 5:110–111, 7:157, 19:29–37).

Some say that Jesus will return in the End Time with the Mahdi. A few say that there is no Mahdi and that only Jesus will return. Others say that the Mahdi will come first and will begin the battle against the *Dadjjal*, the false messiah, and that Jesus will descend later to help him with that battle.

There should be no mistake: the belief that Jesus will return is a belief that he will return as an Islamic Messiah. He will correct the mistaken belief that he is God and will establish Islam as the flowering of the Jewish and Christian traditions. When he comes, both Jews and Christians will realize that they have been wrong and will convert to Islam. There are a few interesting quotes that have been attributed to the Prophet Mohammad in Islamic tradition. According to Abu Hurayrah, Mohammad said:

> All the prophets are brothers. Their mothers are different but their religion is one. I am the first of people with Jesus son of Mary, for there was no prophet between him and me. He will descend. When you see him, you will recognize him to be a man of medium size, with skin of red and white. He has lank hair as if his head is dripping. He will break all crosses, kill the pigs, and abolish the tax on non-Muslims until all who are not under Islam will perish. In his time, God will destroy the Anti-Christ, and will establish security on the earth so that the camel and the lion will graze together, the tiger and the cow, the wolf and the sheep. Children will play with snakes without being

harmed. He will remain for 40 years, then he will be buried and prayed over by Muslims.[4]

This is interesting because it gives a description of Jesus, albeit a not very flattering description. It also says that the Antichrist will be destroyed during his time on earth. This means that according to this prediction he will not arrive in a blaze of glory at the end of the battle of Armageddon, as has been often portrayed, but he will descend to the earth at a time when the battle is still being fought. He will stay only forty years, and will, we assume, be a Muslim.

Ibn Kathir claims that the *hadith* of the Prophet says that:

Jesus will descend on the white minaret in Damascus just as the dawn prayer is happening. This is the easternmost minaret in Damascus which is built of white rock. It was built in the place of the one destroyed by the Christians. Jesus will descend, kill all the pigs, break the crosses, and no one will accept anything but Islam. He will remain for forty years and then he will die and be buried with the Prophet Muhammad and his two companions Abu Bakr and Umar b. al-Khattab.[5]

Again, we find the prediction that Jesus will descend from Heaven, will stay for forty years as a Muslim, and will then die. He will be an advocate for Islam, and he will be given the highest honor of burial with the Prophet.

MODERN VIEWS

There are similarities in these concepts of the Messiah, and those similarities are the main points that most people who believe the

Messiah will return agree on. They believe that he will return after a difficult time, when the forces of evil are raging on the earth and many people have been deceived. As we have seen, we have been through and continue to go through a time of conflict, violence, and natural disaster. Most important, this is a time when many of the major conflicts and some of the most serious tension on the planet are among the three religious groups who are expecting the Messiah: Judaism, Christianity, and Islam. This would be a perfect time for the Messiah to come, and perhaps make a resolution of these conflicts possible that no one involved has even imagined.

There is also agreement that the Messiah will usher in a time of peace, but it is not clear how soon the time of peace will arrive. Many people expect that it will be instantaneous. Jesus or another Messiah will come and take immediate control of the world. He will right wrongs and impose peace in a supernatural way. Other predictions seem to assume that the time of peace will not come so quickly or so easily. Jesus or another Messiah will come and will guide people to the point where a time of peace will be possible.

Another question is how Jesus or another Messiah will arrive. The statement in Revelation 1:13 that the Messiah will be one like the son of man is a reference back to Daniel 7:13–14, where Daniel saw one like a Son of Man come in a cloud to the Ancient of Days. It is important to note that the events in the vision in Daniel were taking place in Heaven at the throne of God, the Ancient of Days. This was not a scene taking place on earth. As we have seen, when New Testament writers use images from the Old Testament, such as references to Babylon or whores, they do not usually mean for those references to be taken literally. John's description of the son of man coming on a cloud is a clear reference back to Daniel, and probably not meant to be taken literally.

It is possible, of course, that Jesus will return on a cloud or will descend in some way. It is also possible that the Messiah will come in a spiritual form that is visible at the time of the spiritual renewal, or that he will be born once again into a physical body. This means that it would not be any easier to recognize him this time than it was last time. People will have to be alert and aware to recognize him when he comes.

The traditional idea is that the Messiah will be a judgmental figure who will crush those who have sided with Satan or with evil. Many find this image hard to fit with Jesus as they know him. Jesus, in the New Testament, is portrayed for the most part as a loving, compassionate person, who places the importance of love above all things. His mission is more one of healing than of condemning. He can be strong and firm, but he is usually kind, patient, nonjudgmental, and forgiving.

It is likely that most Christians, or people in Western culture who have been influenced by Christianity, are expecting the Messiah to be a figure very much like the figure of Jesus in the New Testament. He will guide people to a new understanding and a new way of being in a firm, gentle, and loving way. All we have to do is to know him when we see him.

CHAPTER 14

THE MILLENNIUM OF PEACE

The actual word "millennium" doesn't appear in the Bible. The word comes from the Latin *mille* (1,000) and *annus* (year), and means a thousand-year period of time. This period of time is mentioned six times in Revelation 20:1–7, and this is the source of the expectation of a thousand years of peace. As we have seen, the number 1,000 for the ancients was also a symbolic number meaning a completion and a very large number or a very long time. The one-thousand-year period John refers to in Revelation, therefore, could actually be much longer than a literal one thousand years.

Not all Christians agree on the nature of the Millennium. Some think the rule of Jesus is a spiritual kingdom that has existed since his life on earth over two thousand years ago. This view is called Amillennialism. Others think that the kingdom exists now but there will be a massive conversion to Christianity before the Messiah returns. This is called Postmillennialism. Another group expects a Rapture, or taking up of all good Christians before the final catastrophic events before the Millennium. This, as we have seen, is called Dispensational Premillennialism. And yet another group thinks that all of humanity will be destroyed and only resurrected saints will populate the world during the Millennium. This is called Historical Premillennialism.

Despite all these theories and the debates they engender among theologians, the average Christian expects some kind of period of peace and justice on the earth before the end of the world and the Final Judgment. This is the most straightforward reading of the Book of Revelation and other biblical prophecies. The Book of Revelation does not say that everyone on earth will die before the Millennium. In fact, Revelation 20:4 describes the resurrection of martyrs who will reign with Jesus for one thousand years. It is difficult to see who they would reign over if everyone else was dead.

The most important event John describes for the beginning of the Millennium in Revelation 20:1–3 is the chaining of Satan, the dragon, the serpent, and his confinement to a bottomless pit for one thousand years. Later, in Revelation 20:7, Satan is released and wreaks havoc again. What does this chaining of Satan and casting him into a bottomless pit mean?

In examining the nature of the Beast, we saw that this is the tendency to fight with God or with the whole of existence. The nature of the Beast sets itself up in competition with God and wants to be the Creator instead of a part of creation; it wants to be a separate part instead of an integral part of the whole. This was the nature of Satan when he challenged God in Heaven and was cast down by Michael.

This nature, as we also saw, is very much a human trait. The number of the Beast is 666, and humanity was created on the sixth day of creation. Humanity will always have a tendency toward this trait until it passes through the refining fire of spiritual renewal. Because of this tendency, humanity is susceptible to manipulation by this quality of the Beast. The Bible says that the energy of Satan can delude and control humanity. In other words, people who are motivated by their own lust for power can control other people who cannot see them for what they are. Because the majority of people have not seen the lust for power within themselves, they cannot see it in the Beast figures who arise to control them.

So what does it mean when we say that this Beast energy is restrained but not destroyed during the Millennium? It may mean that a sufficient number of people have reached the level where they can no longer be manipulated by this satanic energy. Not everyone will have reached that level, or the satanic energy would be destroyed completely, but enough may have reached it to prevent the energy from controlling humanity for a very long time.

How do people reach that level of awareness? Prophecy indicates that by following the directions of the universal message contained in the seven letters in Revelation, by following the directions of religious teachings, and by surrendering themselves to the will of God they receive the grace of God and are transformed in the furnace. As the letters to the churches suggest, the dross of their satanic or ego tendencies is burned away, leaving only the pure gold of the Spirit. Some Christians call this sanctity, some other traditions call it enlightenment. Revelation 5:5 says that Jesus is worthy to open the scroll because he has conquered. In the letters to the churches, Jesus urges the congregations to conquer too. Those who conquer will receive great reward.

The Book of Revelation tells us that this spiritual renewal will happen before the Messiah returns, which means that the Messiah and saints will govern a transformed world, and their presence will transform it further. As we have seen, it is possible that the Messiah will be born again in a normal way. The same may be true of the saints who are to govern. In Mark 8:27–30 Jesus asks the disciples who people say he is. They answer John the Baptist, Elijah, and one of the prophets. But Peter says he is the Messiah. This text does not mean that people think Jesus is literally the resurrected John the Baptist, Elijah, or some other prophet, but that he has their nature. So it is possible that the resurrection in Revelation refers to this kind of return of the saints.

On the other hand, since Christians understood that Jesus had risen bodily from the dead, they may have expected others to literally do the same. Jesus rose from the dead shortly after death and before his body had decayed. Saints who have been dead some time will no longer have bodies to return to, and John may have meant that these saints will have spiritual bodies, that new physical bodies will be created for them, or that their old bodies will return. However they return, Revelation says that they will rule for a very long time.

BIBLICAL TIME OF PEACE

What will life on earth look like if a significant number of people have been transformed and live their lives according to the will of God, if the leaders are all saints, or transformed people, and if the Messiah himself is directly involved in ruling the earth? The Old Testament gives us some idea:

> *The word that Isaiah the son of Amoz saw concerning Judah and Jerusalem.*
>
> *And it shall come to pass in the last days, that the mountain of the LORD's house shall be established in the top of the mountains, and shall be exalted above the hills; and all nations shall flow unto it.*
>
> *And many people shall go and say, Come ye, and let us go up to the mountain of the LORD, to the house of the God of*

Jacob; and he will teach us of his ways, and we will walk in his paths: for out of Zion shall go forth the law, and the word of the LORD from Jerusalem.

And he shall judge among the nations, and shall rebuke many people: and they shall beat their swords into plowshares, and their spears into pruninghooks: nation shall not lift up sword against nation, neither shall they learn war any more.

O house of Jacob, come ye, and let us walk in the light of the LORD.

Therefore thou hast forsaken thy people the house of Jacob, because they be replenished from the east, and are soothsayers like the Philistines, and they please themselves in the children of strangers.

Their land also is full of silver and gold, neither is there any end of their treasures; their land is also full of horses, neither is there any end of their chariots:

Their land also is full of idols; they worship the work of their own hands, that which their own fingers have made:

And the mean man boweth down, and the great man humbleth himself: therefore forgive them not.

Enter into the rock, and hide thee in the dust, for fear of the LORD, and for the glory of his majesty.

The lofty looks of man shall be humbled, and the haughtiness of men shall be bowed down, and the LORD alone shall be exalted in that day.

For the day of the LORD of hosts shall be upon every one that is proud and lofty, and upon every one that is lifted up; and he shall be brought low (Isa. 2:1–12).

First many people gather in a form of spiritual renewal. Then peace is brought to the people through arbitration. The King James

Version above uses the word "rebuke" (Isa. 2:4), but the New Revised Standard Version, considered by most scholars to be a more accurate translation, says, "He shall judge between the nations, and shall arbitrate for many peoples" (Isa. 2:4). This means that a wise judge will resolve difficulties through fairness and arbitration.

What will follow is a time of peace in which the resources of war will be used to care for people—swords will be beaten into plowshares and spears into pruninghooks. The United Nations estimates that if just a portion of the resources used to create weapons was used for food and housing, no one on the planet need be homeless or hungry. Because a fair judge will resolve the issue that makes people so fearful that they want weapons to protect themselves, there will no longer be a reason to waste resources in this way. Humanity will be free to use the earth's resources to care for everyone on the planet.

Next, materialism will be exposed for the petty thing it is. Our greed, our desire for more and more material things, our conceit about what we have created, will all be put into perspective in the greater scheme of things. There is nothing wrong with material comfort, but the driving lust for material things, and our conceit in what we can do, can be very destructive. By putting everything in its proper place, these skills can be used, not for greed or control, but to create beauty and productivity for everyone. All this happens under the guidance of the Messiah and those who have conquered.

As these changes happen, more and more people will realize that the desire to fight with God is destructive, and they too will come to surrender their lives or egos to God. Isaiah 11 gives us more information about this peaceful kingdom:

And there shall come forth a rod out of the stem of Jesse, and
a Branch shall grow out of his roots:

And the spirit of the LORD shall rest upon him, the spirit of wisdom and understanding, the spirit of counsel and might, the spirit of knowledge and of the fear of the LORD;

And shall make him of quick understanding in the fear of the LORD: and he shall not judge after the sight of his eyes, neither reprove after the hearing of his ears: But with righteousness shall he judge the poor, and reprove with equity for the meek of the earth: and he shall smite the earth: with the rod of his mouth, and with the breath of his lips shall he slay the wicked.

And righteousness shall be the girdle of his loins, and faithfulness the girdle of his reins.

The wolf also shall dwell with the lamb, and the leopard shall lie down with the kid; and the calf and the young lion and the fatling together; and a little child shall lead them.

And the cow and the bear shall feed; their young ones shall lie down together: and the lion shall eat straw like the ox.

And the sucking child shall play on the hole of the asp, and the weaned child shall put his hand on the cockatrice' den.

They shall not hurt nor destroy in all my holy mountain: for the earth shall be full of the knowledge of the LORD, as the waters cover the sea (Isa. 11:1–9).

In this text we see the coming of the Messiah, and he is once again portrayed as a fair judge who does not judge from the mind or the emotions, as most people tend to do, but judges from a higher spiritual level that is based in a submission to the will of God. The result of this is a kind of peace that is almost beyond our ability to understand. We have believed that there are such things as natural enemies. The wolf is the enemy of the lamb, and the viper is the enemy of the child, but we will come to a new kind of understanding, where we can live in complete peace every day. In the process of creating this peace, the Messiah also rights economic wrongs. The meek and the poor will receive equity—their fair share. Without extreme economic injustice that creates resentment and dissension, true peace is possible. The peace between humans and various animals portrayed here probably also means that the environment will be treated with respect, and there will be a peaceful coexistence between humanity and the rest of the earth.

Again, in the last verse, there is a reference to a spiritual renewal, where the earth is full of the knowledge of the Lord. We saw from Isaiah 2:2 that this begins before the Messiah comes but continues and grows under his just rule and the time of great peace.

The Book of Revelation gives us another clue as to how the earth is to be governed by references to the twenty-four elders. They first appear in Revelation 4:4 dressed in white robes and seated on twenty-four thrones. We know that in Revelation white robes signify those who have been purified or cleansed. The twenty-four are repeatedly shown falling before God and Jesus (Rev. 5:8, 11:16, 19:4). This demonstrates that they are not subject to the Beast energy of rebellion against the will of God, but are completely surrendered to God and indicates that their rule will be the rule of God's will.

This is a major change from how the earth is governed now. The people who hold positions of political power are very rarely people who are considered great, wise, spiritual leaders. We have tended to compartmentalize the separation of Church and State to the extent that truly wise people stay away from politics. John indicates that in the Millennium all of this will change. People will be chosen to govern based on their wisdom, their level of refinement, and the extent to which they are surrendered to the will of God or to the whole of existence.

So the Millennium, which may be a longer time than one thousand years, will be a time of spiritual renewal, peace, justice, equity, productivity, and peaceful coexistence with the environment. It will be a time of government by the wise in the spirit of God.

Unfortunately, this will not last. The energy of Satan, the desire for separate personal power, will still remain in the world. In some way—probably because people will begin to forget the horrors of the past and want to satisfy their greed and lust for power without realizing what horrible destruction that energy can bring—enough people on the earth will be susceptible to the delusion of Satan, and the Beast energy will rise one last time. This will culminate in a final battle, and the energy of Satan will be destroyed forever.

We don't know if this final battle between good and evil will happen in the old way of war that we now know, or if it will be a battle on another level, where the Messiah and the transformed people finally manage to battle the creature/ego element in humanity and defeat it forever through universal consciousness.

CHAPTER 15

WILL IT HAPPEN IN OUR TIME?

Old Testament prophecies, such as Ezekiel 36–38, set out a basic plan leading to the End Time. Israel will be gathered together again, there will be an invasion of Israel in which her enemies will be defeated in a miraculous way, and the Messiah will return. The Old Testament does not give us any reliable timelines for these events.

There is a Dispensationalist belief that there will be a seven-year Tribulation period after the Temple in Jerusalem is rebuilt. At some point during that time, the saints on earth will be taken in a "rapture" up to Heaven. At the end of the battle of Armageddon, during which everyone else will be killed, these saints will return to the earth with Jesus for the Millennium. This scenario has been popularized by the *Left Behind* series of novels by Tim LaHaye and Jerry B. Jenkins. The official Dispensationalist rational for this theory is a combination of Old Testament and New Testament scriptures that critics say cannot reasonably be read together. The concept of the Rapture is based on texts most Christians think refer to resurrection.

FORTY-TWO YEARS

We have seen that the Book of Revelation uses the number seven often, but John doesn't use that number for any time period. There are two references to time periods in Revelation. The first is Revelation 11:2, which says that there is no need for John to measure the court outside the Temple, because the nations will trample it for forty-two months. The next reference to time is in Revelation 11:3, which says that the two witnesses of God will prophesy for 1,260 days. The last reference to time is in Revelation 13:5, where the beast-nation is allowed to exercise authority for forty-two months. Forty-two months is three and a half years in either a lunar year of 360 days or a solar year of 365 days. If we use a lunar year of 360 days, then 1,260 days is also three and a half years.

The first period mentioned, the trampling of the courtyard of the Temple, seems to be consistent with the other reference to forty-two months, the rule of the beast-nation. In other words, these seem to be two references to the same event. There is no reason to add those together to make seven years, as some commentators seem to do. The linking of the desecration of the courtyard and the rule of a Beast takes us back to Daniel 9:27, a prediction that is linked to the End Time by Jesus (Matt. 24:15; Mark 13:14). The language in Daniel is that a desecration of the Temple will happen for half a week. This has been interpreted as half a week of years, or three and a half years. As we saw, the prediction in Daniel that the Temple would be desecrated for three and a half years was fulfilled by Antiochus Epiphanes in 169. He had pigs slaughtered on the altar for a period of three and a half years, the same period of time that he ruled. This makes it likely that the time of rule and the time of desecration are the same time period.

John used the forty-two-month time period in Revelation, which is the literal equivalent of three and a half years. That linked his prophecy to Daniel, because John's readers would have interpreted the half a week in Daniel 9:27 as three and a half years. If John literally meant three and a half years and wanted to be consistent with Daniel, he would have used the same figure Daniel used: half a week. But John did not do that. He used the figure forty-two instead. Why link the text to Daniel and then use a different number?

We have already seen that in biblical discussion of time, numbers can refer to different time units other than the ones given: days, weeks, months, years, weeks of years. When John used the figure forty-two, he most likely meant forty-two years or forty-two week of years, which is 294 years. The forty-two weeks links the prediction to Daniel and tells us that this is a continuation of ancient biblical prophecy. The number forty-two gives us a time period different from the one in Daniel. This would mean that there would be forty-two years or 294 years of difficulty after some significant event in the End Time scenario.

In little more than half of the last century we saw the following series of events: A beast-nation in the form of Fascism arose. Three nations—Germany, Italy, and Japan—allied themselves around this philosophy and attempted to take over the world. The leading figure in Fascism was Adolph Hitler, an Austrian, who is associated with the number 666 and who attempted to have himself declared the new Messiah, to destroy Judaism, and to replace Christianity with his own religion. Millions died in the conflict, in which tons of bombs were dropped, including firebombs and two atomic bombs dropped on Japan by the United States. The conflict did tremendous damage to the environment as well as to people. The Fascist Axis powers were defeated by what Nostradamus told us could only be divine intervention.

Three years after the end of that war, a Jewish state was created, which later became the nation of Israel. Israel had to fight for its survival. In 1967, Israel was invaded by an alliance of Middle Eastern countries. A significant battle of that war was fought in Meggido. Israel won a victory in six days that shocked the world. This became known as the Six Day War, assuring the survival of Israel. Internal conflict with the Palestinians, whose ancestors held the land for over a thousand years before the creation of Israel, continues to create an atmosphere of danger and insecurity.

In the rest of the world since the end of World War II, the Cold War manifested itself in a series of deadly conflicts, and the death toll for the last half of the century was larger than the death toll for the Second World War. In addition, industrialization, cars, and war tactics have resulted in serious damage to the environment, which is causing global warming and the destruction of the rain forest, which produces the oxygen we need to survive. Terrorism has increased, and nuclear proliferation means that atomic weapons are spread around the world with a potential to destroy the planet several times over. AIDS has killed millions, bacteria are mutating so that they can't be treated with antibiotics, and earthquakes and other natural disasters have killed people in record numbers.

We see a beast-nation, the Axis alliance; an Antichrist, Adolf Hitler; the gathering of Israel from the nations in the formation of the nation of Israel; an invasion of Israel with a battle in Megiddo, and an amazing victory by Israel in the Six Day War; and we see a period of catastrophic events. Since the battle of Megiddo, the apocalypse or time of tribulation has continued for thirty-six years so far. Many commentators believe the Six Day War is an important event in this scenario, because, even if the Megiddo battle was not the Armageddon referred to in Revelation, the gathering of Israel after the destruction of the nation and of Jerusalem over eighteen hundred years before was a momentous event. It was only after the Six Day War that anyone could say that Israel had definitely returned as a nation.

Forty-two years from the Six Day War gives us the year 2009, and we believe this is a critical date. This may be the date by which humanity has to choose between another round of Beast, Antichrist, war, and Apocalypse—an alternative prediction of several prophets—or choose a spiritual renewal and the return of the Messiah. If humanity chooses war at this time, the result may be that the Messiah will not return for two hundred and ninety-four years.

All the events outlined in the Bible leading to the return of the Messiah have already happened. Whether or not a spiritual renewal has happened that is large enough to merit the return of the Messiah remains to be seen. If a spiritual renewal of sufficient magnitude is now under way or takes place in the next few years, we could see the return of the Messiah in some form in or around the year 2009.

OTHER PROPHECIES

Reports of a Last Pope Other prophecies agree with this timing. Several prophets, including Nostradamus, have prophesied the end of the Catholic papacy in a short time from now. What better reason would there be for the papacy to end than the return of the Messiah? The pope is considered by Catholics to be a kind of regent or caretaker who has a role only if God is not present on earth.

In the twelfth century, an Irish bishop named Mael Maedoc Morgair helped bring the Roman Catholic liturgy to Ireland. A renowned healer, prophet, and miracle worker, he was later canonized as Saint Malachy. In 1130 he made a pilgrimage to Rome to have an audience with Pope Innocent II. At his first sight of the city, he had a vision of all the popes to come until the end of the line of popes, which he recorded as "Prophetia de Futuribus Pontificis Romanis." These prophecies were stored in the Vatican archives and forgotten until 1596, when they were published by a Benedictine monk. Mallachy said there would be a succession of 112 popes, and he described each one in a rhyme. The present pope from Poland is pope number 110. Pope John Paul II is now in his early eighties and in ill health. The next two, and last, popes are described by Mallachy as "Gloria Olivae" and "Petrus Romanus." The previous pope, John Paul I, lived only a few months after his selection, so it is very possible that there could be two more popes by the year 2009.

On May 13, 1917, three shepherd children saw a beautiful woman come out of the sky and speak to them. She told them to return on the thirteenth of every month, which they did for the next six months. Her message is that war is a punishment for evil, but if people would pray and repent their sins, peace would be granted. "If my requests are granted . . . there will be peace." She predicted the outbreak of World War II several decades later and predicted the Russian revolution by atheists. She promised that on her last visit she would perform a miracle so that people would believe her message.

On October 13, 1917, the lady appeared to the children for the last time. She gave them a secret message that had three parts. The first two parts have been revealed for some time. The first was a horrible vision of hell. The second was a request for the pope to consecrate Russia to her. "If my requests are not granted, Russia will spread its errors throughout the world, raising up wars and persecutions against the Church. The good will be martyred. The Holy Father will suffer much and various nations will be annihilated." The third part of the message remains controversial. The last living seer wrote it down and gave it to the Vatican in 1957, saying that it could be made public after 1960.

Despite this permission, the text was read by each successive pope but not released until 2000. At that time, the Vatican released what it claimed was the text of the final vision. The vision involved a scene in which many people, including Catholic religious, lay dead. A figure in white, who the children thought was the pope, walks shakily through this scene and then is gunned down by soldiers and shot with arrows.

The Vatican denies that this is an apocalyptic vision, arguing that the dead in the vision represent the Christians who have been persecuted in the last century and the shooting of the pope was a prediction of the shooting of Pope John Paul II by a Turkish man, Ali Agca, in 1981.

Both the Church's interpretation and the authenticity of the text released have been questioned. Father Paul Kramer of the Fatima Centre in Fort Erie, Ontario, publicizes his doubts on the fatima.org website. He believes that part of the third prediction has not been revealed, and his website contains a petition that he asks others to send to the pope, asking that the full vision be revealed. Father Kramer claims that Sister Lucia has said that the final prediction was apocalyptic:

> To someone who was questioning her on the content of the *Third Secret*, Sister Lucy one day replied: "It's in the Gospel, and in the Apocalypse, read them." She has also confided to Father Fuentes that the Virgin Mary has made her see clearly that "we are in the last times of the world." This does not mean, one must emphasize, the time of the end of the world and of the last judgement, since the triumph of the Immaculate Heart of Mary must come first. Cardinal Ratzinger him-

self, discreetly alluding to the content of the Secret of Fatima,
has mentioned three important elements: "The dangers threat-
ening the faith," "the importance of the last times" and the fact
that the prophecies "contained in this Third Secret correspond
to what has been announced in Scripture." We even know that
one day Lucy indicated Chapter 8 and 13 of the Apocalypse.[1]

The Vatican's interpretation of the vision is also questionable on
the basis of the vision revealed by it, since the pope figure in the vision is shot by several soldiers and not by one civilian. Further
doubt has been raised by a forensic report from a laboratory in
Michigan, which compared the text released by the Vatican with
samples of Sister Lucia's writing over a period of fifty years. The laboratory concluded that the writing in the Vatican text could not be
identified as the writing of Sister Lucia.[2] A question remains, therefore, whether entire text or the correct text of the final vision has
been revealed.

The three children who saw the vision were Lucia, Francisco,
and Jacinta. Francisco and Jacinta died in the flu epidemic in 1918.
Lucia became a nun and is still alive today.

Reports have long indicated that the third prediction relates to
the last pope, though this is not the Vatican's interpretation. The
predictions given to the children at Fatima were to be fulfilled
within the lifetimes of the three children. Lucia is in her late
nineties. She says that Mary told her in a vision that she would stay
in the world for a very long time. By the year 2009, she will be over
one hundred years old. Perhaps we will know more about what the
final vision foretold.

Other Prophecies There are two other predictions that could help
place the return of the Messiah in our time. According to Dr. Jose

Arguelles, an expert on Mayan cosmology, the Mayan elders of today expect a change of a great cycle to occur in the year 2012. This is a change that has been expected for over three thousand years. The new era that will come in will be characterized by non-materialism, the development of technology in harmony with the environment, and a new kind of government,[3] a description remarkably consistent with equally ancient prophecies for the Millennium from the Hebrew Bible.

Gautama Buddha, the inspiration and great teacher of Buddhism, predicted in the *Diamond Sutra,* twenty-five centuries ago, that there will be a radical change of consciousness with accompanying periods of intense chaos every twenty-five hundred years, and that a teacher will come to give the wheel of Dharma a push at that time. The time of change he was predicting was to happen at the beginning of the twenty-first century.

The Age of Aquarius As we saw in chapter 2, the Age of Aquarius has the characteristics described in the Bible for the Millennial age: an emphasis on unity and coming together, peace, and good use of resources. It also closely resembles the age that has been predicted by the Mayan elders for the past three thousand years. We have also seen that the number 1,000 is not necessarily exact and can mean a longer time: It could mean that the Millennium can last the entire Age of Aquarius.

We are now experiencing a time of transition and turmoil. History tells us that the beginning of the Piscean Age was also tense, chaotic, and frightening, and we can safely assume that every change of astrological age involves difficult and unsettling changes. We can anticipate that a future change to an Age of Capricorn will be equally unsettling and might account for an expectation of discord to arise after a very long time of peace.

There is a certain amount of disagreement about when the Age of Aquarius begins, but many place the date on the spring equinox in the year 2000. Since the point of the astrological ages moves backwards through the signs of the zodiac, that means that we are in the last degree of Aquarius, and will remain there for approximately seventy years.

A form of astrology called the Sabian Symbols, presented in Marc Jones's book *The Sabian Symbols in Astrology*,[4] and popularized by the great astrologer Dane Rudhyar in his 1936 book *The Astrology of Personality*,[5] gives us an interesting insight. This system gives a meaning for each degree of the zodiac, and the meaning for the last degree of Aquarius is very interesting:

> *This symbol speaks to spiritual integrity, and to the basic friendliness of the universe. The image of the field of Ardath in bloom, or Marie Corelli's mystic meadow of ancient Babylon, is poetic testimony to the ability of seeds and ideas sown far in the past to maintain their identity and purpose, and to survive and flourish through many lifetimes. Implicitly in this image of blossoms in an ancient field is an allusion to group consciousness and the sustainment of the invisible brotherhood. On a practical level, this image symbolized liveliness, inspiration and those soul-refreshing moments that renew hope and remind an individual of the good in the world and himself.[6]*

Like the expectations of the Millennium, this speaks of friendliness and coming together, the development of group consciousness, a continuity with wisdom of the past, and the wisdom of the past coming to flower in a time of hope and renewal. All of this is consistent with the possibility of the return of the Messiah.

John, in the Book of Revelation, gave us the number forty-two, which is not likely to refer to a period of three and a half years or seven years but to a period of forty-two years. The most significant event of our time related to biblical prophecy is the victory of Israel in the Six Day War. This was the fulfillment of ancient biblical prophecy after a break of eighteen hundred years, and something many people didn't believe possible. If we add forty-two to 1967, we get the year 2009 as a significant year.

This may be the year when the world makes its final choice between war or the return of the Messiah. On the other hand, time may be even shorter for humanity to choose. The year 2009 may be the year of the Messiah's actual return, either through a human birth in that year or through a return in some other way. When humanity is ready, the Messiah will return. The question now is "Will it happen in our time?"

CHAPTER NOTES

INTRODUCTION

1. C10 V72—this citation is from Nostradamus' most famous book, *Centuries*. The book is divided into numbered "centuries," which include a number of verses. So this is a citation from century 10, verse 72.
2. Hal Lindsey, *The Late Great Planet Earth* (Grand Rapids, MI: Zondervan, 1970), 20.

CHAPTER 1
AN OVERVIEW OF PROPHECY

1. "Church History: The Revelation of the Coming," www.churchhistory.net/ articles/mm/html.
2. Ibid.
3. "So what is the key to Dispensationalism?" Endtimes.org.
4. "What about the Dispensations?" Ibid.
5. "Doctrinal Statement, Article 3: Angels, Fallen and Unfallen." This is the doctrinal statement of the Dallas Theological Seminary, the leading institution for Dispensationalist theology, available online at Endtimes.org and other Dispensationalist sites.
6. Ibid.

CHAPTER 2
ASTROLOGY AND MYTH IN THE BIBLE

1. David Fideler, *Jesus Christ, Sun of God: Ancient Cosmology and Early Christian Symbolism* (Wheaton, IL: Quest Books, 1993), 23.
2. Ibid., 6.

3. Lester Ness, *Written in the Stars: Ancient Zodiac Mosaics* (Warren Center, PA: Shangri-La Publications, 1999), 83, 91.

4. Ibid., 144.

5. Ibid., 152.

6. Manly P. Hall, *The Secret Teachings of All Ages* (Los Angeles: Philosophical Research Society, 1994), 196.

CHAPTER 3
THE SECRET OF NUMBERS IN THE BIBLE

1. "The Stones Cry Out" [online] www.stonescryout.com.

2. David Fideler, *Jesus Christ, Sun of God* (Wheaton, IL: Quest Books, 1993), 371.

3. Fideler, *Sun of God,* 53.

4. Plato, *Republic,* 527B. In *The Republic of Plato.* Translated by Francis MacDonald Cornford (New York: Oxford University Press, 1941).

5. Fideler, *Sun of God,* 25.

6. Proclus, *The Commentaries on the Timaeus of Plato,* II. Translated by Thomas Taylor. 2 vols. (Hastings: Chthonios, 1988), 77.

7. Proclus, "On the Sacred Art." In *On the Mysteries,* edited by Stephen Ronan (Hastings: Chthonios, 1989), 146.

8. Gallileo. In John Robinson, *An Introduction to Early Greek Philosophy: The Chief Fragments and Ancient Testimony with Connecting Commentary* (Boston: Houghton Miffin, 1968), 69.

9. Origen, *Contra Celsum,* 1.79. Translated by Henry Chadwick (Cambridge: Cambridge University Press, 1980).

10. Clement of Alexandria, *Stromata or Miscellanies,* 5.9. In *Ante-Nicene Fathers,* II, 458.

CHAPTER 5
BABYLON THE BEAST

1. John J. Collins, *Apocalypticism in the Dead Sea Scrolls* (London, N.Y.: Routledge, 1997), 13.

2. J. Ramsey Michaels, *Interpreting the Book of Revelation* (Grand Rapids, MI: Baker Books, 1992), 45.

3. Lynn Louise Schuldt, *Prophecy Paradox: The Case for a First Century End Time* (Concord, CA: Son Mountain Press, 1996), 165.

THE SECOND BEAST: THE ANTICHRIST

1. Walter C. Cambra, *Gog and Magog: A Study in Thematic Clarification*, ms. Graduate Theological Union Library, Berkeley, California, 14.
2. David Haggith, *End-time Prophecies of the Bible* (New York: G. P Putnam's Sons, 1989), 133–34.
3. Schuldt, *Prophecy Paradox: The Case for a First Century End Time* (Concord, CA: Son Mountain Press, 1996), 174.
4. Suetonius, Tranquillus, *DeVita Caesarum,* Book 6, quoted in Schuldt, 174.
5. Haggith, *End-time Prophecies,* 279.
6. Schuldt, *Prophecy Paradox,* 169–170.
7. Gerard Bodson, *Cracking the Apocalypse Code: The Shocking Secrets of the Book of Revelation Decoded* (Boston: Element, 2000), 29.
8. Collins, *Apocalypticism in the Dead Sea Scrolls* (London, NY: Routledge, 1997), 57–100.
9. F. Aster Barnwell, *Meditations on the Apocalypse: A Psycho-Spiritual Perspective on the Book of Revelation* (Rockport, MA; Shaftsbury, Dorset; Brisbane, Queensland: Element, 1992), 81.
10. Walter C. Cambra, *Gog and Magog: A Study in Thematic Clarification*, ms. Graduate Theological Union Library, Berkeley, California, 136.
11. Schuldt, *Prophecy Paradox,* 93.
12. Haggith, *End-time Prophecies,* 275.
13. Bodson, *Cracking the Apocalypse Code,* 85–87.
14. Haggith, *End-time Prophecies,* 275–77.
15. Bodson, *Cracking the Apocalypse Code,* 51.
16. Haggith, *End-time Prophecies,* 133–35.
17. *Ignatius to the Magnesians,* V., "Early Church Fathers" [online] www.ccel.org/fathers/ANF-01/igna/ig2magnesianslong.html.
18. Peter Lorie, and Liz Greene, *Nostradamus, the Millennium of Beyond: The Prophecies to 2016* (London: Bloomsbury, 1993), 75.
19. Peter Lorie, *Your Personal Guide to the Year 2000: The Millennium Planner* (London: Boxtree, 1995), 78.

CHAPTER 7
JESUS AND THE BEAST

1. Fideler, *Jesus Christ, Son of God,* (Wheaton, IL: Quest Books, 1993), 59, 69.
2. Plato, *Republic,* in *The Republic of Plato.* Translated by Frances MacDonald Cornford (New York: Oxford University Press, 1941), 4430–440, 142.
3. Fideler, *Sun of God,* 62.
4. John Michell, *The Dimensions of Paradise: The Proportions and Symbolic Numbers of Ancient Cosmology* (San Francisco: Harper & Row, 1988), 180.
5. Ibid., 182.

CHAPTER 8
APOCALYPSE

1. Haggith, *End-time Prophecies of the Bible* (New York: G.P. Putnam's Sons, 1989), 210–11.
2. Ibid., 186.
3. *Chicago Tribune,* 25 Oct., 1998.
4. "Infoplease.com," www.infoplease.com/ipa/A0884804.html.
5. Matthew White, "Historical Atlas of the Twentieth Century," users.erols.com/mwhite28/20centry.htm, citing a Dec. 20, 1999, press release from a large reinsurance company, Munich Re.
6. Bodson, *Cracking the Apocalypse Code* (Boston: Element, 2000), 147.
7. "15th Field Artillery Regiment," www.landscaper.net/agent.htm.
8. "Agent Orange Victim Fund," www.vnrc.org.vn/orange.fund.html.

CHAPTER 9
GOG AND MAGOG IN THE BATTLE OF ARMAGEDDON

1. Eric H. Cline, *The Battles of Armageddon: Megiddo and the Jezreel Valley from the Bronze Age to the Nuclear Age* (Ann Arbor: University of Michigan Press, 2000), 1.
2. Ibid., 182.

3. M. M. Pickthall, *The Meaning of the Glorious Qur'an: Explanatory Translation* (Amana Publications: Beltsville, MD, 1996).
4. Maulana Muhammad Ali, *The Antichrist & Gog and Magog* (Lahore: Ahmadiyyah Anjumn Isha'at Islam, 1976), 6 n.12.
5. Ibid., 7.

CHAPTER 10
ISRAEL AND THE TEMPLE

1. "Temple Mount & Eretz Yisrael Faithful Movement," www.templemount-faithful.org.
2. Ibid.
3. William Patterson. "Seeds of the Antichrist." *The Gurdjieff Journal* (Vol. 8, I, 29): 28.
4. Haggith, *End-time Prophecies of the Bible* (New York: G. P. Putnam's Sons), 1989), 100.
5. Ibid., 96.

CHAPTER 11
THE END TIME

1. Gregg Braden, *The Isaiah Effect: Decoding the Lost Science of Prayer and Prophecy* (New York: Harmony Books, 2000), 61.
2. Cayce reading #311-10. In Braden, *The Isaiah Effect*, 64–65.
3. This consecration is controversial. Some claim that because it consecrates the world, and not just Russia, to the Immaculate Heart, it is not sufficient to fulfill the request. Others claim that Sister Lucia, the one remaining seer of Fatima, wrote a letter to Sister Mary of Bethlehem, saying that the 1984 consecration fulfilled the Lady's request, because the bishops of the world joined in the consecration, as they had not done with the consecrations in 1942, 1967, and 1982. Sister Lucia confirmed this in a letter to Father Robert J. Fox in 1990.
4. Timothy Tindal-Roberton, *Fatima, Russia, and John Paul II* (Still River, Mass.: 1992).
5. "The End Days," www.webcom.com/enddays/events.html.

6. Haggith, *End-time Prophecies of the Bible* (New York: G. P. Putnam's Sons, 1989), 211.

CHAPTER 12
SPIRITUAL RENEWAL

1. J. Ramsey Michaels, *Interpreting the Book of Revelation* (Grand Rapids, MI: Baka Books, 1992), 36.
2. F. Aster Barnwell, *Meditations on the Apocalypse: A Psycho-Spiritual Perspective on the Book of Revelation* (Rockport, Mass.; Shaftsbury, Dorset; Brisbane, Queensland: Element, 1992), 85.
3. Ibid., p. 111.
4. *Didache,* Chapter XVI. In Schuldt, *Prophecy Paradox,* 164.

CHAPTER 13
THE MESSIAH

1. Collins, *Apocalypticism in the Dead Sea Scrolls* (London, New York: Routledge, 1997), 71.
2. Geza Vermes. *The Dead Sea Scrolls in English Read and Extended,* 4th edition. (London and New York: Penguin, 1995), 113.
3. Shi'I Islam is the second-largest sect, comprising 10 to 15 percent of Islam. Sunni Islam is the largest sect. The Mahdi also appears in Sunni Islam, though he does not have the same eschatological significance that he has in the Shi'I tradition.
4. Brannon M. Wheeler, *Prophets in the Quran: An Introduction to the Quran and Muslim Exegesis* (London, New York: Continuum, 2002), 317.
5. Ibid., 317.

CHAPTER 15
WILL IT HAPPEN IN OUR TIME?

1. "The Fatima Network: Our Lady of Fatima Online," fatima.org.
2. "Speckin Report on Alleged Third secret," www.tldm.org/news/speckin-p1.htm.

3. Braden, *The Isaiah Effect: Decoding the Last Science of Prayer and Prophecy.* (New York: Harmony Books, 2000), 55.

4. Marc Edmund Jones, *The Sabian Symbols in Astrology* (Santa Fe. N.M.: Aurora Press, 1993).

5. Dane Rudhyar, *The Astrology of Personality* (Garden City, N.Y.: Doubleday, 1970).

6. Diana E. Roche, *The Sabian Symbols: A Screen of Prophecy* (Victoria, BC: Trafford Publishing, 1998), 364.

BIBLIOGRAPHY

BOOKS AND MAGAZINES

Arthur, David. *A Smooth Stone: Biblical Prophecy in Historical Perspective.* Lanham, N.Y.: Oxford: University Press of America, 2001.

Barnwell, F. Aster. *Meditations on the Apocalypse: A Psycho-Spiritual Perspective on the Book of Revelation.* Rockport, Mass.; Shaftsbury, Dorset; Brisbane, Queensland: Element, 1992.

Bodson, Gerard. *Cracking the Apocalypse Code: The Shocking Secrets of the Book of Revelation Decoded.* Boston: Element, 2000.

Braden, Gregg. *The Isaiah Effect: Decoding the Lost Science of Prayer and Prophecy.* New York: Harmony Books, 2000.

Brownlee, William Hugh. *The Meaning of the Qumran Scrolls for the Bible; With Special Attention to the Book of Isaiah.* New York: Oxford University Press, 1964.

Cambra, Walter C. *Gog and Magog: A Study in Thematic Clarification,* ms. Graduate Theological Union Library, Berkeley, California.

Clement of Alexandria, *Stromata or Miscellanies,* 5.9 in *Ante-Nicene Fathers,* II, 458.

Cline, Eric H. *The Battles of Armageddon: Megiddo and the Jezreel Valley from the Bronze Age to the Nuclear Age.* Ann Arbor: University of Michigan Press, 2000.

Collins, John J. *Apocalypticism in the Dead Sea Scrolls.* London, New York: Routledge, 1997.

Evans, Craig, and Peter W. Flind, eds. *Eschatology, Messianism, and the Dead Sea Scrolls.* Grand Rapids, MI, Cambridge, U.K.: William B. Eerdmans Publishing, 1997.

Fideler, David. *Jesus Christ, Sun of God: Ancient Cosmology and Early Christian Symbolism.* Wheaton, IL: Quest Books, 1993.

Haggith, David. *End-time Prophecies of the Bible.* New York: G. P. Putnam's Sons, 1989.

Hall, Manly P. *The Secret Teachings of All Ages.* Los Angeles: Philosophical Research Society, 1994.

Jones, Marc Edmund. *The Sabian Symbols in Astrology.* Santa Fe, N.M.: Aurora Press, 1993.

Lindsey, Hal. *The Late Great Planet Earth.* Grand Rapids, MI: Zondervan, 1970.

Lorie, Peter, and Liz Greene. *Nostradamus, the Millennium of Beyond: The Prophecies to 2016.* London: Bloomsbury, 1993.

Lorie, Peter. *Your Personal Guide to the Year 2000: The Millennium Planner.* London: Boxtree, 1995.

Maulana Muhammad Ali. *The Antichrist & Gog and Magog.* Lahore: Ahmadiyyah Anjumn Isha'at Islam, 1976.

Mays, James Luther, and Paul J. Achtemeier, eds. *Interpreting the Prophets.* Philadelphia: Fortress Press, 1987.

Michaels, J. Ramsey. *Interpreting the Book of Revelation.* Grand Rapids, MI: Baker Books, 1992.

Michell, John. *The Dimensions of Paradise: The Proportions and Symbolic Numbers of Ancient Cosmology.* San Francisco: Harper & Row, 1988.

Ness, Lester. *Written in the Stars: Ancient Zodiac Mosaics.* Warren Center, PA: Shangri-La Publications, 1999.

Origen, *Contra Celsum,* 1.79. Translated by Henry Chadwick Cambridge: Cambridge University Press, 1980.

Patterson, William. "Seeds of the Antichrist," *The Gurdjieff Journal* (Vol. 8, I, 29): 28.

Pickthall, M. M., *The Meaning of the Glorious Qur'an: Explanatory Translation.* Amana Publications: Beltsville, MD, 1996.

Plato, *Republic,* 527B in *The Republic of Plato.* Translated by Francis MacDonald Cornford. New York: Oxford University Press, 1941.

Proclus, "On the Sacred Art," in Stephen Ronan, ed., *On the Mysteries.* Hastings, U.K.: Chthonios, 1989.

Proclus. *The Commentaries on the Timaeus of Plato,* II. Translated by Thomas Taylor, 2 vols. Hastings, U.K.: Chthonios, 1988.

Robinson, John. *An Introduction to Early Greek Philosophy: The Chief Fragments and Ancient Testimony with Connecting Commentary.* Boston: Houghton Miffin, 1968.

Roche, Diana E. *The Sabian Symbols: A Screen of Prophecy.* Victoria, BC: Trafford Publishing, 1998.

———. *The Sabian Symbols: A Screen of Prophecy.* Victoria, B.C.: Trafford Publishing, 1998.

Rudhyar, Dane. *The Astrology of Personality.* Garden City, N.Y.: Doubleday, 1970.

Schuldt, Lynn Louise. *Prophecy Paradox: The Case for a First Century End Time.* Concord, CA: Son Mountain Press, 1996.

Tindal-Roberton, Timothy. *Fatima, Russia, and John Paul II.* Still River, MA: 1992.

Vermes, Geza. *The Dead Sea Scrolls in English Read and Extended,* 4th edition. London and New York: Penguin, 1995.

Wheeler, Brannon M. *Prophets in the Quran: An Introduction to the Quran and Muslim Exegesis.* London, New York: Continuum, 2002.

ON THE WEB

"Agent Orange Victim Fund," www.vnrc.org.vn/orange__funddocument.html.

"Doctrinal Statement, Article 3: Angels, Fallen and Unfallen," Endtimes.org.

"Early Church Fathers," www.ccel.org/fathers/ANF-01/igna/ig2magnesianslong.html.

"The End Days," www.webcom.com/enddays/events.html.

"15th Field Artillery Regiment," www.landscaper.net/agent.htm.

"Historical Atlas of the Twentieth Century," users.erols.com/mwhite28/20centry/htm.

"Infoplease.com," www.infoplease.com/ipa/A0884804.html.

"So what is the key to Dispensationalism?" Endtimes.com.

"Speckin Report on Alleged Third Secret," www.tldm.org/news/speckin-p1.htm.

"The Fatima Network: Our Lady of Fatima Online," fatima.org.

"The Stones Cry Out," www.stonescryout.com.

"Temple Mount & Eretz Yisrael Faithful Movement," www.templemountfaithful.org.

"What about the Dispensations?" Endtimes.com.

INDEX

ABOUT THE AUTHOR

Peter Lorie spent much of his teen years in the Far East. He was educated as a lawyer, and in the early 1970s turned to writing and publishing. During this time he traveled throughout India and the Far East, where he met with Krishnamurti, Osho, and Da Free John as well as many others of the lesser-known spiritual masters of the twentieth century. He also lectured to thousands of people in the U.S. on subjects related to prophecy. His books include four titles on Nostradamus, which sold over 3 million copies worldwide, books on the prophesies of the Bible, including those in Revelation, and also "histories" of the future, which derived from the great non-biblical works of the past. *World's End: 2009* has evolved from a lifetime of discovery and research.

He is the father of two grown-up children, and has lived for extensive periods in Tibet, India, New York, Italy, and London and now lives in California, where he is currently working on several new studies of prophetic writing.